FROM FEAR TO FAITH

FROM FEAR TO FAITH

Studies of Suffering and Wholeness

EDITED BY

NORMAN AUTTON

LONDON

S · P · C · K

1971

First published 1971
by S.P.C.K.
Holy Trinity Church
Marylebone Road
London N.W.1

Printed in Great Britain by
The Camelot Press Ltd, London and Southampton

© Norman Autton, W. A. Lishman,
Anthony Bloom, John Hinton, C. Murray Parkes,
C. F. D. Moule, Ian Ramsey, 1971

ACKNOWLEDGEMENTS

Thanks are due to the following for permission to quote from copyright sources:

Blackfriars Publications: *The Pain of Christ and the Sorrow of God*, by Gerald Vann.

A. and C. Black Ltd.; *The Freedom of the Will*, by Austin Farrer.

SBN 281 02605 X

CONTENTS

CONTRIBUTORS

W. A. Lishman, B.SC., M.D., M.R.C.P., D.P.M., is Senior Lecturer in Psychiatry in the Institute of Psychiatry of the University of London.

Archbishop Anthony Bloom, M.D., is Metropolitan of Sourozh and Exarch for Western Europe.

John Hinton, M.D., B.S., F.R.C.P., D.P.M., is Professor of Psychiatry at the Middlesex Hospital.

C. Murray Parkes, M.D., D.P.M., is Consultant Psychiatrist at the Tavistock Institute of Human Relations.

C. F. D. Moule, D.D., F.S.A., is Lady Margaret Professor of Divinity at Cambridge University.

Ian Ramsey, D.D., is Bishop of Durham.

THE EDITOR, Norman Autton, M.A., is Director of Training of the Hospital Chaplaincies Council, Church House, Westminster.

Introduction

Norman Autton

Daniel Defoe, in a memorable passage in his *Adventures of Robinson Crusoe*, describes Crusoe's attempts to instruct Friday "in the knowledge of the true God". In the course of the instruction he tells Friday that "the devil was God's enemy in the hearts of men, and used all his malice and skill to defeat the good designs of Providence, and to ruin the kingdom of Christ in the world, and the like. 'Well,' says Friday, 'but you say God is so strong, so great; is He not much strong, much might, as the devil?' 'Yes, yes', says Crusoe, 'Friday; God is much stronger than the devil— God is above the devil, and therefore we pray to God to tread him down under our feet, and enable us to resist his temptations, and quench his fiery darts.' 'But', says he again, 'if God much stronger, much might as the wicked devil, why God no kill the devil, so make him no more do wicked?'" Completely taken aback at such a question, Crusoe reflects, "after all, though I was now an old man, yet I was but a young doctor, and ill enough qualified for a casuist, or a solver of difficulties; and at first I could not tell what to say; so I pretended not to hear him, and asked him what he said."[1]

There is still a tendency today to shun Friday's question, couched though it may be in differing forms and in varying language. Pain, suffering, death, and bereavement, the subjects of this symposium, are all aspects of the mystery of evil in a God-created world. Fortunately it is not a mystery which is enshrouded

[1] *The Adventures of Robinson Crusoe*, Daniel Defoe. J. M. Dent & Sons 1963, pp. 162–3.

in complete darkness, for there are great shafts of light "which
the darkness has never mastered" (John 1.5). With Friday many
today seek for enlightenment, but are either put off by seemingly
cut-and-dried solutions or find that their real questions are not
answered because, as with Crusoe, there is the tendency "not to
hear".

It was in order to grapple with these and kindred problems
that the Hospital Chaplaincies Council invited a number of those
who are engaged in the helping and healing professions to
Church House, Westminster, during the autumn of 1969 to hear
the views of and to enter into dialogue with a number of well-
known theologians, psychologists, and psychiatrists. Unfortunately two of the original contributions could not be published
in this symposium. The first was that dealing with "The Psychology of Guilt", by Dr William Kraemer, M.D., Dr David Howell,
M.B., B.CH., B.SC., D.P.M., and Dr Rosemary Gordon-Montagnon,
PH.D., three analytical psychologists of the Jungian School.
Each adopted a different approach to the whole subject of guilt,
thus stimulating most fruitful discussion and audience participa-
tion. It may be helpful therefore to recall some extracts. Dr
Kraemer showed that guilt must be acknowledged, understood,
digested, and borne, rather than disregarded or denied. We may be
tempted to use magic and try to get rid of it, but what then will
happen to us and our capacity to feel responsibility? What about
our growth as individuals and social beings? Yet help is badly
needed to cope with such guilt lest we be crushed by it or make it
barren by displacement or escape. It is just here that pastor,
psychologist, and psychiatrist have a common bond. Man is a
creature who stands in need of being held, whether he be a moon-
farer or a very small baby; whether he sees himself as omnipotent
or impotent, whether or not he knows of his inner guilt experiences. The necessity for a real holding relationship outshines
all else, and this real relationship is first encountered with his
mother. Priests and analysts continue where she, the mother, has
left off or fallen short, and the aim must be the individual's
growing ability to relate to others, to depend and be dependable,
and to be aware of this inner and outer world in which guilt
looms so large.

The "scapegoat" aspect of guilt feelings was dealt with by Dr
Howell, illustrated by the Gospel story of the woman taken in

adultery, where the scribes and Pharisees projected their own guilt on to the woman, taking advantage of the public exposure of her guilt to disown their own. They "being convicted by their own conscience" had, as a result of Jesus' challenge, to take it back into themselves and own it consciously. Dr Rosemary Gordon-Montagnon made it plain that the capacity to feel guilty was an achievement and as such was crucial for the development of both individual and social maturity. The importance of realizing the difference between "shame" and "guilt" was also emphasized, and the distinction was defined in the following terms. Shame is concerned with the impression one thinks one makes on others: with being looked at and discovered to be smaller or weaker, more ineffectual or more ridiculous than one would like to be. Shame is centred on vision. Guilt, on the other hand, can be experienced even when one is all by oneself, when nobody watches, when nobody speaks except that small inner and often relentless voice of conscience. The presence of guilt is a sign that, as Winnicott has suggested, the stage of concern has been reached. Greed and destructiveness will have to confront and do battle with the feelings of loving and caring *within* the individual himself. Emphasizing the unpleasant components of the experience of guilt, Dr Gordon-Montagnon yet showed how it is an essential prerequisite for the development of consciousness, the acceptance of conflict, the sacrifice of omnipotence, and the assumption of personal identity and personal responsibility. For the search to repair what one has damaged opens up the possibility of change, of growth, and the exploration of one's creative resources.

The other contribution which is not included is "The Theology of Death" by Professor John Hick. Most fortunately this is now available in a companion publication, *Dying Death and Disposal* (ed. Gilbert Cope. S.P.C.K.). Suffice it to say here that it makes essential reading as providing an excellent study of one of the major themes included in the *From Fear to Faith* symposium.

Before we can minister at all adequately to those in pain we have to understand some of the psychological and psychiatric implications involved, for in our eagerness to help we can so easily hinder; in our readiness to serve we often find it difficult when our theology has to be held in abeyance and our impulsive need to reassure and smooth things over put aside. Methods and techniques soon prove of minor importance, for our prime concern is the extension of a relationship, an identification with the patient in the very depths of his predicament. Dr Lishman describes very vividly the various ways in which people react to severe prolonged pain. With such understanding and insight our sensitivity in the exercise of pastoral care can be sharpened, and our presence at the bedside symbolize a real loving, understanding, and caring concern. We have all felt on various occasions moments (which seem like hours) of inadequacy, so crippling and inhibiting. What Dr Lishman has to say concerning the emotional reactions of those who witness pain deserves the most careful and serious study. The present writer recalls some words of Fr Gerald Vann, o.p. in this connection. He is writing of the stillness of Mary at the foot of the cross:

It is a terrible thing, a thing we must all at some time have suffered, that feeling that someone you love is suffering and you can do nothing to help. . . . Be still: the stillness and the silence of Mary are the signs not of defeat but of intense and creative activity. There are times when outward busyness only makes matters worse, when, *though it may bring you yourself relief*, it must be for the other at best ineffectual and at worst an additional exacerbation of suffering. Be still . . . there is nothing that Mary can do or say; no, but they have no need of words, her son and she; it is love that heals. And so, when . . . you want to do something for the pain and sorrow, you want to comfort, never think that there is nothing you can do. Think deeply and love deeply and then you will have no need of words: your sympathy, your co-suffering, will go straight from your own heart to the heart of Christ.[1]

In a world which seeks to avoid pain and suffering at any cost there is the tendency to see only the wastefulness and the purposelessness of it all. "Why this waste?" (Matt. 26.8). "That eternal 'why' . . . that question mark twisted like a fish-hook in the human heart." With Archbishop Anthony Bloom we are brought face to face with real-life situations which have led not only sufferers, but also those who have been privileged to witness such suffering, to greater spiritual depths. There is a French saying, "Souffrir passe, avoir souffert demeure éternellement"—"Suffering passes, to have suffered abides for ever". Here is no theoretical

[1] *The Pain of Christ and the Sorrow of God*, Gerald Vann, o.p. Blackfriars 1947, pp. 33–4 (italics mine).

theology, but rather the theology of the prison, persecution, and concentration camp. Here is the witness of men and women who were not prepared to be mere suffering idealists, no mere victims of fate but rather victors in glory. These are they who "had to face jeers and flogging, even fetters and prison bars" and whose "weakness was turned to strength" (Heb. 11.34, 36). These are they who knew with Blake that "God is . . . even in the depths of Hell". It was such a spirit that prompted Teilhard de Chardin, whose sister lay seriously ill, to ponder—"Margaret, my sister! While I, devoted to the positive forces of the universe, was travelling continents and oceans, passionately concerned to see all the colours and beauties of the earth, you were lying there, stretched out motionless, transforming in your innermost being the worst darkness of the world into light. In the sight of God, our Creator—tell me—which of us had the better part?"[1] It was such a spirit that moved Malcolm Muggeridge "into a kind of ecstasy" when faced with a person at the point of death among the pilgrims at Lourdes, whose "eyes were quite fabulously luminous and beautiful", prompting him to say, "It was as though I saw God's love shining down on us visible, in an actual radiance."[2]

Professor John Hinton and Dr C. Murray Parkes deal with the subjects of the dying and the bereaved, and readers may already be familiar with their writings on these topics. Until fairly recently both death and bereavement have been most neglected areas of pastoral and psychiatric concern. Significant philosophical contributions to the subject of death were made in the 1920s by Heidegger, a metaphysician, Ehrenberg, a biologist, and Freud, a psychiatrist. It is Tagore who reminds us that "life as a whole never takes death seriously. It laughs, dances, and plays, it builds, hoards, and loves in death's life." Death, "the great adventure", has become the "king of terrors". The attempt to conceal if not to ignore the threat of "non-being" is both ancient and modern, for the wheel seems to have turned full circle. We learn from John Donne that the ancient Romans could not name death even in their wills. They would not say "Si mori contigerit", but "Si quid humanitus contingat"—not "if, or when, I die", but "when the course of nature is accomplished upon me". In modern times we hear John Betjeman asking:

[1] Quoted in *Pain and Providence*, Ladislaus Boros. Burns & Oates 1966, p. 66.
[2] *Jesus Rediscovered*, M. Muggeridge. Fontana Books 1969, p. 118

Oh why do people waste their breath
Inventing dainty names for death?
(*Churchyards*)

There seems a basic conviction of invulnerability in most of
us which prompts us to believe that nothing bad can happen to us
personally—death comes to others, not to me; other people
become sick, I don't. It can't happen to me!

As with those in pain, so too in ministering to the dying and
the bereaved, it is essential that we be familiar with some of the
emotional factors involved. What are some of the needs of the
dying and the bereaved? How best can they be met? How do we
handle the so-called "conspiracy of silence" with the dying, and
the social and cultural tabu which still stifles the full expression of
grief of the bereaved? What influence has religious faith when
associated with the anxieties of the dying and the sorrow of the
bereaved? Both lecturers deal with these and other factors which
are of common concern to pastor and psychiatrist. It is hoped that
these questions will lead the reader to further study of current
medico-moral problems such as the prolongation of life which
impinges on the two issues of dying and bereavement. One is
reminded of Miss Taylor, the elderly patient in the chronic ward
described in Muriel Spark's novel *Memento Mori*, who reflects,
"For my part I would be glad to be let die in peace. But the
doctors would be horrified to hear me say it. They are so proud
of their new drugs and new methods of treatment—there is
always something new. I sometimes fear, at the present rate of
discovery, I shall never die!"

The theology of the nature of man must be studied before
there can be an effective co-operation between Church and
medicine. Jean-Paul Sartre's modern man has lost his sense of
sin, and there can be no redemption won by cheap grace, no
matter how much a world which craves for a "religion without
tears" is anxious to gain satisfaction. Dietrich Bonhœffer in
The Cost of Discipleship makes this abundantly clear. "Grace is
costly because it cost God the life of his Son. 'You were bought
with a price' (1 Cor. 6.20), and what cost God much cannot be
cheap for us." As Friday was "too earnest for an answer to forget
the question", Crusoe, after much thought and prayer, "entered
into a long discourse with him upon the subject of the redemption
of man by the Saviour of the world, and of the doctrine of the

gospel preached from Heaven, viz, of repentance towards God and faith in our blessed Lord Jesus."[1] We too were led on to a theology against which to place the various problems which the series had set out to discuss and in which the various professions represented might find common ground. We were most fortunate to have both Professor C. F. D. Moule and the Bishop of Durham as our mentors for the study of forgiveness and wholeness. The former deals with the "compensatory" aspect of forgiveness and invites us to work out with him such questions as, "Since forgiveness is a free but costly gift, and repentance no less costly, is there then, after all, a transaction involved? Is it a matter of barter? Are quantitative ideas to be applied in order to analyse the process of forgiveness and reconciliation?" The latter, after commenting upon Descartes' psychophysical concept of man as a dualistic being of "body" and "mind", and Aristotle's teaching in his *De Anima*, leads us on to inquire how medical science itself comes to think in terms of unities, in terms of "wholeness". It is just here that we reach the heart of the discussion. Is our theology able to supply an interpretative scheme which is coherent with medicine's unity of personality and concept of wholeness and set it within the Christian perspective? It is to this theme that the Bishop devotes the second half of his lecture.

It is only when such fundamental issues have been explored and an adequate theology formulated that we progress from *fear*, "tossed by the waves and whirled about by every fresh gust of teaching", to *faith* and "knowledge of the Son of God—to mature manhood, measured by nothing less than the full stature of Christ" (Eph. 4.13, 14).

[1] op. cit., p. 163.

1

The Psychology of Pain

W. A. Lishman

Pain is a subject with which we all feel intensely familiar. It forms an integral part of life's experiences, we have all felt it from time to time, and at first sight we tend to feel that we know about it only too well. But in fact it is an extremely complex part of man's experience, and one which produces many puzzles and unsolved challenges. It involves all aspects of man, the physical, the psychological, and the spiritual. Specialists in all these areas have important things to say about pain. I shall deal mainly with the psychological and psychiatric aspects since that is my own profession.

First I shall outline what we know of the mechanisms involved in feeling pain. I hope to show that the perception of pain is no simple mechanical situation, but one that involves important emotional components which can influence very powerfully the amount of suffering involved. Then I want to show that these emotional components are built into our personalities in a very fundamental sense, probably quite early on in life. As a result of this the emotional constitution of the person feeling the pain, and the setting in which it occurs, can have important effects. We shall move on to consider the various ways in which people react to severe prolonged pain. Those of you who work in hospitals will be very familiar with some of these. I shall then outline briefly the way in which pain is used for communication with people around, and finally attempt to deal with the very complex and difficult subject of psychogenic pain, which is pain occasioned by mechanisms of the mind alone, not by any damage to the body.

MECHANISMS INVOLVED IN PAIN PERCEPTION

This is a subject which illustrates very well that any dichotomy between the mind and the body is false. When we are thinking of the mechanisms behind pain, we are forced to realize that in every pain sensation there are physical and mental components, which are inextricably bound together.

The Physical Component is a matter of electrical nerve impulses which travel along nerve fibres to the brain and there produce the signal that "pain has occurred". Not one of us can define or communicate just what that feeling is, for it is entirely personal and private. It is worth noting at the outset that even this physical basis for pain is not a simple or straightforward matter. The parts of the brain which deal with pain are not clearly understood. We know a good deal about the organization of the brain for dealing with other sensations—touch, hearing, vision, and so on—but we cannot locate with precision the higher centres which deal with pain. Yet obviously the pain sensation must get to the highest centres, so that we can understand what is causing the pain and take appropriate action. There are other puzzles too. Sometimes, in very severe painful states that cannot be cured, surgeons will attempt to cut the nerves, or the tracts of nerve fibres in the spinal cord, in order to prevent the pain sensations arriving at the brain. This can be dramatically successful, but every now and then we see peculiar cases in which these operations fail. A patient may suffer physical pain originating in his leg, the tracts can be completely destroyed, and yet the pain comes back again a few weeks later. This is seen strikingly in some cases of "phantom-limb" pain. When patients have a leg amputated they may have a "phantom leg" which remains: in other words, they feel their leg is still there. Sometimes they suffer excruciating pain in the leg which is no longer there and, no matter how much the surgeon tries to destroy any possible pain pathways, the pain continues. Such cases provide dramatic examples of how pain can defeat the ordinary physical laws, and show us that pain sensation cannot be regarded as something which is totally and purely a mechanical problem of nerve impulses.

An Emotional Component always exists as well as the physical component in pain perception. How important is this? Can it actually influence the severity of the pain perceived? How much do we have to think about it when we are dealing with people in pain? Any consideration of the emotional component plunges us right away into those complex and difficult matters, areas of human emotions, attitudes, and expectations. Let us first of all note that pain is never described to us in neutral terms, but always in a most feeling way. In fact none of us, however stoical we may feel we are, can be neutral and objective about our own pain. Pain always manages to stir up very powerful feelings. This leads us to suspect that the emotional constitution of a person is going to be important in determining how much he suffers from the pain experience. It also suggests that the setting, from one experience to another, will have important effects in any one person. In fact every pain experience has so many variables attaching to it that it will be unique. A few examples will illustrate these points.

THE SETTING IN WHICH THE PAINFUL EXPERIENCE OCCURS

Montaigne in the sixteenth century wrote: "We feel one cut from the surgeon's scalpel more than ten blows of the sword in the heat of battle." This is a very valid observation. There have been very careful studies done, and it seems that a surgical operation, creating as it does a certain amount of tissue destruction, is liable to be followed by more pain than a much bigger wound inflicted on a soldier in battle. For the surgical patient the setting is one of anxiety, the whole situation a cause for dismay and distress. For the soldier on the field of battle there is something honourable about the wound, sometimes even an honourable release from ever present danger. Certainly it has been found that in general the soldier genuinely makes less complaint and requires less in the way of pain relieving drugs than does the average surgical patient.

Let us now turn to the patient already in hospital for surgical operations. Careful studies have been made of groups of people all undergoing equivalent operations. In one such study every alternate patient was treated rather specially, was told carefully in advance about the pain he would feel, where he would feel it, for how long, and how bad it would be. The mechanisms behind it were fully and carefully explained to him. When the operation was over, these patients were visited every day and given simple encouragement and reassurance. The other group of patients were put through the operation in the ordinary way without the special briefing. The result was clear. The patients who had been properly prepared had much less pain than the others. The nurses themselves did not know which patients were in the special group, but were found to have given them less in the way of pain relieving drugs. Independent observers, rating the amount of objective distress, confirmed that these simple psychological manœuvres had had a definite effect in lessening the pain produced. It even emerged that the specially prepared group were on average discharged much earlier from hospital. Thus the management of psychological situations can do much to modify the amount of pain which is felt, and such lessons are increasingly incorporated into good ward practice.

A more dramatic example is provided by the extraordinary phenomenon of hypnosis. You may have seen the parlour trick in which a person under hypnosis is told that his arm is without feeling, and then the flesh is pierced right through. People susceptible to hypnosis sometimes can have teeth extracted or even more painful procedures carried out in an hypnotic trance. Now there is no indication that under hypnosis the physical apparatus for pain is altered in any way whatsoever. Pain impulses are getting along nerves and to the brain in just the usual way. Hypnosis acts purely in the psychological sphere to modify the second emotional component to pain perception. We have here a vivid illustration of just how important the emotional component can be. Of course when dealing with hypnosis we are dealing with a very abnormal mental state. But if psychological factors can totally abolish pain, we must logically be prepared to believe that they can also do the reverse. We will later be discussing situations in which pain is felt, and genuinely felt, without objective cause.

The operation of prefrontal leucotomy provides another example as dramatic as hypnosis. This consists of cutting tracts of brain tissue in the frontal lobes of the brain, and can occasionally be successful in preventing suffering in some very painful conditions which cannot be treated by other means. It is an operation which must only be used very cautiously indeed because it is liable to have other undesirable effects, but it can in favourable cases take away all the emotional reaction to pain. The patient may still say he can feel his pain if this is enquired about, but he is not distressed and he does not show evidence of suffering. It seems that the operation has cut across the ability to develop and sustain that second emotional component which is so important a part of the total pain experience.

THE INFLUENCE OF PERSONALITY ON PAIN

This can be studied quite scientifically by testing the "pain thresholds" in different groups of people. Having secured willing volunteers for your experiment, you very gently apply a painful stimulus and increase it until the first painful reaction is noted. For example, you can slowly increase pressure on a part of the body until it begins to hurt, or increase the intensity of a tiny beam of radiant heat until the first scorching sensation is felt. These are among the many different ways of measuring the pain threshold. As you might expect, manual workers such as miners have higher thresholds than office workers, no doubt because they have become habituated to minor abrasions of the body and thus their pain apparatus has probably become more tolerant. Men have slightly higher thresholds than women. Different races also vary somewhat in their pain thresholds. But the greatest differences in pain threshold turn out to be connected, not with physical but with psychological factors.

Extroverts for instance have higher pain thresholds than introverts. Anxious people have much lower thresholds than calm people, and indeed anxiety turns out to be one of the most powerful factors influencing pain thresholds. The pain threshold is lower in fatigue and higher when people are feeling fresh and active. This is a very important observation because pain itself is fatiguing, so with long continued pain one gets a progressive lowering of the threshold as a result. Patients suffering from neurotic disorders are found in general to have low pain thresholds. Patients who are constantly worrying about their health, in particular the so-called hypochondriacs, have very low thresholds indeed. Thus it appears that where certain types of mental constitution are concerned, the sensitivity to pain is definitely increased. The total apparatus for pain, physical and emotional, is set to trigger off and sense painful perceptions more readily and more severely.

In a similar way when the pain has reached a certain degree one can measure how long a person can bring himself to go on tolerating it. This "pain tolerance threshold" is again found to be influenced by the various personality factors outlined above.

This emotional component is obviously very intricately embedded in personality and is probably built in and conditioned quite early in life. One has only to think of a child and his intense psychological reaction to every painful experience to realize how closely this must get woven into other aspects of his developing emotional life. His pattern of response to pain will become shaped by his own individual needs, and by the demands and prohibitions of the family. Think also of the powerful reactions his pain will call forth from the people around him. When he falls down and hurts his knee, for example, he will usually become enveloped in maternal care, comfort, and concern. When he is older and needs to express the powerful aggressive feelings of childhood, he soon finds that pain can be meted out as well as received by way of revenge and punishment. The important emotion of guilt is early and deeply associated with pain, and the two continue to be linked as personality development proceeds. Of course as we go through life each painful experience will condition us to react slightly differently to the next; more than with any other sensation our reaction to it becomes progressively coloured by previous experiences and by anticipation of consequences. The result is that as adults we have our special "pain personality" which is unique to each of us and which will give the individual stamp to our emotional reactions to pain.

At this point it is interesting to look back and see what Aristotle thought of pain, because he did not put it with the sensations—sight, hearing, taste, touch, and smell. He classed pain with the "passions of the soul". In other words, for Aristotle pain was a powerful *emotion*, not a *sensation* at all.

THE PATIENT'S REACTION TO PAIN

So far we have been rather theoretical and experimental. I want now to look at the various ways in which people react when they are suffering from painful illnesses.

At the outset I wish to stress how tremendously important it is when dealing with sick people to be aware of the complex emotional state as well as the physical state of the patient in pain. Pain should never be seen as a physical problem alone. Good doctors and nurses have always known this and have reacted as though by instinct to the whole person in pain. The person who is suffering pain will not wish merely to communicate an abstract piece of information to the doctor, nurse, or priest. He will not baldly state "I have pain", but he will want to communicate all sorts of things about what the pain is doing to him, how it is affecting him, what it means to him, and what he wants his listener to do in return.

With acute pain and with chronic pain the effects are rather different. When in acute pain the patient is not aware at first of anything except the intensity of the overwhelming experience. As the pain begins to die away, however, he becomes aware of shock, surprise, dismay, or anger. He can look around and see what is causing the pain and try to take some action to stop it happening again. Most important of all, he can put a certain psychological distance between himself and the pain. It then becomes something outside of him, and he can deal with it, examine it, and decide how to cope with it. Chronic continuing pain, especially pain which arises internally, is a different matter. There is no object to look at or avoid, nothing external about which to feel angry. There is no immediate action which the patient can take to protect himself. The psychological distance between the patient and the pain is minimal; he feels invaded, trapped, and occupied by the pain. It is no longer just a matter of having a hurt body, but he is a hurt body in totality. In this situation the painful feeling tends to crowd out everything else and cannot be ignored, and so no rest or respite can be found. In a long continued severely painful illness the mental and physical resources of the patient become exhausted, and inevitably he begins to think less logically, less sensibly, and in a less adult way than at more normal moments. Those of you who have been through long lasting painful experiences will probably be able to bear this out. It is only the most resolute and rare personality that can withstand the effects of chronic severe pain without this element of irrational and childish thinking taking place. Let us now look at some of the results.

The commonest reaction to severe pain is *anxiety*, and what worse reaction could there be in view of what we know about the effects of anxiety on lowering pain thresholds? With persistence of pain, the imagination very readily runs ahead to fear the worst. As a result we often get a vicious circle in which the pain causes anxiety and the anxiety aggravates the pain. It is essential to try to combat this emotion when ministering to those in pain. Communication with the patient should be as good as possible, so that unreal fears are kept to a minimum. This is, of course, the well-known medical problem of how much to tell, to whom, and when. It is particularly distressing to find that patients in hospital learn so many partial truths through ward gossip, or half-hear and misconstrue the comments made on ward rounds. This can be highly dangerous and damaging to the patient with a chronic painful illness. In addition to proper communication—and it may sound trite to say it—it is also very important for all who look after the patient to have a confident and a thoroughly caring attitude. Once this confidence is established it serves to combat anxiety very powerfully.

Those of you who work in hospitals will also know that *anger and resentment* can figure very prominently indeed in the presence of chronic pain. This, like anxiety, is a natural first response to the presence of pain. With long continued and unrelenting pain resentment can easily progress to feelings of persecution. The pain intrudes persistently, cannot be ignored, and it is hard to distract oneself from it or compensate in other ways. C. S. Lewis in the *Problem of Pain* says, "God whispers to us in our pleasures, speaks in our consciences, but shouts in our pains." Again he says "Pain is unmasked, unmistakable evil." In response to this tyrannical aspect of pain, the patient comes to feel bedevilled and persecuted. He finds it hard to accept that his body is letting him down, and projects the blame elsewhere. Thus he may come to think, "Look what everybody is doing to me. Why am I being treated like this?" Or he may say, and you may have heard this very often, "What have I done to deserve this suffering?" When such questionings continue the patient often becomes extremely bitter and comfort cannot easily be transmitted. Those around are cast in the role of parents who have failed when needed or, even worse, as parents who cannot possibly care. Such patients need the utmost tact and patience if they are to be gently guided towards acceptance of the true situation.

A feeling of being *forsaken* is another common reaction when in this intolerable situation. It is probably true to say that we are never quite so alone as when we are in severe pain. Relationships come to feel rather distant, and some patients, particularly those who have been rather dependent people, may come to feel unloved and abandoned. In consequence they cling tenaciously to relationships with those around, and may come to seek attention in all sorts of ways in their attempts to feel that they do after all belong. It is important to realize that just "being there" can give great comfort, and not to withdraw when we feel we have done all we can.

This feeling of being forsaken may progress to feeling worthless and deserving to be abandoned. This is the *depressive reaction* helped on by the questioning thought, "What have I done to deserve this pain?" So often people try to look for adequate causes when they are in trouble, and a person in the throes of a painful illness will often begin to examine himself and dwell upon his wrong doings with increasing guilt. He will try to seek some action on his part to account for what has happened, and may well begin to feel that he has deserved and brought on the pain himself. There are some people, of course, who feel very guilty whenever they are totally dependent upon others. They rely on being the giver and the doer to ward their guilt away. These are the people again who may become extremely depressed in the course of a very painful illness.

We have, too, the other responses in which the patient under stress harks back to childhood types of reaction. This is referred to in psychological terminology as "regression". In one form of regression the patient attempts to revert to being the centre of all concern. He is again like a small child to whom everybody must give attention and whose every demand must be satisfied immediately. This is the *egocentric response* of the chronic invalid in pain. He becomes petulant, overconcerned with every symptom, jealous of attention given elsewhere, and hard to pacify, no matter how much is done for him. It is an understandable reaction, for it is a basic form of self-preservation, but it is one that provides great difficulty in management. Alternatively regression may take the form of troublesome *passivity*, with abandoned weeping, total dependency on those around, and unceasing demands for help. If such patients sense they are being pushed away as a result of their behaviour they of course regress even further, and the whole situation is often one which is very difficult to treat.

I have not mentioned the good reactions to severe pain. This is not because they do not occur, for we have all seen the brave, remarkable responses of some people in such conditions. Such people are fortunate, but I have rather wanted to dwell on the less fortunate and how best they can be helped.

THE RESPONSE OF PEOPLE WITNESSING PAIN

In addition to the sufferer's own response, we must briefly consider the response of those around. We see in fact much the same gamut of emotions. Anxiety is understandable and inevitable, but as we have seen must be controlled and, when at all possible, masked from the patient. The natural desire to "do something" must issue in a calm approach to action. Calmness and confidence are very contagious emotions.

Feelings of guilt are easily lit up in those who witness someone in pain. Relatives often look back with sorrow to things that have happened in the past, and sometimes the guilt is projected on to the doctors and nurses who are thought not to be doing all they might or trying hard enough to help.

A feeling of impotence is of course often prominent in all who are concerned with the person in severe pain. Sometimes there seems nothing more that can be done. We all have to learn something of the acceptance of our limitations, and realize that we do in fact fail our patients quite often. It is comforting to remember that, when we have done all we can, there is always a little more we can do by just being there, or seeing that someone is there, so that the person is not bereft of fellowship and companionship. Dr Cecily Saunders, who has such wide experience of patients in very severe pain, once asked a patient what he looked for above all in those who were caring for him. He replied "for someone to look as if they are trying to understand me". He did not say that he wanted someone who would do things, but rather to know that someone was trying to understand how he felt, and what he was going through. This is a moving illustration of what remains to be done through personal relationships, when other techniques of treatment have at last done all they can.

COMMUNICATION ASPECTS OF PAIN

Like any other emotion, a pain response is a means of relating to and communicating with other people. This emerges most clearly if we look at cases in which a disproportionate amount of distress is occasioned by a given pain-producing situation; in other words, when we see a patient in whom we think pain is being exaggerated. If we enquire carefully and get to know the person well, very often we can discover certain needs or purposes which the pain is in fact fulfilling. If I give you a few examples, I am sure you can multiply them from your own experience.

Some such people are living very lonely and isolated lives. Their complaints of pain are in effect often a way of saying "Don't leave me, take pity on me and stay close." This is a message that rings through many a lonely person's complaints of pain. Again, think of the woman living at home with a painful illness and a husband who is not caring very much, or who has treated her badly in the past. Quite often her complaints of pain contain an element of revenge, and are saying in effect, "See how much I suffer, and think what you have done to me in the past: think of what you are doing to me right now." Complaints of pain are sometimes a form of expiation for guilt, and behind them lies the message, "Look how bravely I suffer and forgive me for my transgressions in the past". Sometimes the pain is serving to take the mind off other troublesome issues which are thereby forced to hang fire—"I am too distressed and troubled to deal with that now". Again sometimes the patient is saying to his doctor, "I have a secret fear that there is something a great deal more serious that you haven't yet spotted. Please redouble your efforts and make sure that you are not missing something". These are very basic messages which the pain complaint is conveying in indirect form. These patients are not wishing consciously to mislead, but are doing something which is common in human behaviour—expressing a need of which the person is only dimly aware by a means outside of conscious control. They are not verbally expressing what they really want, but the subconscious mind is allowing it to come across by a roundabout route.

We have strong reason to believe that the pain in these situations *is* felt to be worse when it can fulfil a need or purpose, and that these psychological factors can truly aggravate the severity of the pain experience. We have probably all experienced this within ourselves in varying degrees. A painful corn may suddenly assert itself when one is obliged to turn from a pleasant to an uncongenial task; a chronic toothache may intensify when difficulties arise in the course of the day's events. I think it is a genuine observation that pain feels worse when there is a setting or purpose in which its being worse will in some way fulfil a function. This being so, for many patients in chronic pain we have to tune ourselves in to listen to any other messages which are coming across along with the complaints of the pain itself. Unless we attempt to deal with the true message, the complaints are likely to intensify, and we are not going to give the person the help he needs. We must try to hear the total message, deal with the total problem, and help the patient to talk about the basic problem rather than about the pain which is sometimes merely the vehicle of distress.

PSYCHOGENIC PAIN

We have been dealing above with a certain type of pain, namely pain which is aggravated by psychological factors. This is an example of "psychogenic pain". Other varieties of psychogenic pain result directly from the effects of emotions on the body, for example some headaches which in tense and anxious persons may be the result of muscular tension in the scalp itself. But finally I wish to mention a third variety of psychogenic pain which we can perhaps name the "psychogenic pains proper".

These are pains which are caused *totally* and *entirely* by psychological factors, and in which there is no organic damage or change in any part of the body. In other words, psychological mechanisms are themselves giving rise to pain without the need of any peripheral stimulus. What evidence is there to support this notion of purely psychogenic pain? First there are certain very rare, very sensitive individuals, who apparently can experience pain by merely thinking certain thoughts, or by imagining certain situations. Others can develop genuine pain by sympathetic mechanisms when witnessing severe pain in others. Freud reported an interesting case of a man who was helping to straighten his brother's hip joint, and at the moment when the joint cracked into place he himself developed severe pain radiating down his leg. I do not know how many of you who work in hospitals have felt the pain of your patients on odd occasions, but such experiences do occur.

Now there is nothing new in experiencing something which does not exist objectively. We all know about hallucinations. And even under normal circumstances we can dream and see things that are not really there. It should, therefore, not be too surprising that perfectly ordinary people can develop and experience pain when there is no objective cause for it.

We have already seen how pain comes closer than other sensations to being an emotion. Certain emotional states, in particular aggression, depression, and guilt, seem to be closely involved with psychogenic pain. Professor Stengel reported a patient with a phantom limb which became unbearably painful whenever he saw or heard of injury or any act of violence. Many television programmes portraying aggression and violence would bring on agonizing pain. This patient was so sensitive to the threat of pain by violence that he reacted as if it were happening to him. In another very interesting case, reported some thirty years ago by Eisenbud, a man with psychogenic headache was hypnotized and under the hypnotic trance certain false ideas were implanted in his mind. He was, for instance, told that a certain nurse in his hospital ward had accused him groundlessly of theft. When he was woken from the trance his behaviour was carefully observed. Though he had no memory of the false idea, it was noticed that dealings with this particular nurse regularly brought about his customary headaches; the other nurses on the ward produced no such effect. After a few days he was rehypnotized and the false idea removed from his subconscious mind. No further headaches were thereafter produced by this particular nurse. We might, of course, frown somewhat upon the ethics of this experiment. But it shows us clearly how resentment and hostility, even that deriving from sources of which the patient may not be fully aware, can sometimes be intimately associated with psychogenic pain.

Depression, too, is associated with psychogenic pain. Sometimes when talking to a patient with pain one is impressed by the vagueness of the description of the pain, yet also with the intensity of suffering which is going on. We suddenly become aware that the patient is severely depressed, and realize we are dealing with a painful emotion state, rather than a painful limb or abdomen. Some people find it very hard to admit to being depressed, and all of their misery becomes channelled into the psychogenic pain. When one eventually gets to the heart of the problem, the pain gradually ceases to be mentioned. Many dramatic cures of psychogenic pain have been made by means of antidepressant treatment in such situations.

It is not only depression and aggression that are related to psychogenic pain, though these are perhaps the most obvious emotional states related to it. Psychoanalysts who learn to enquire very deeply and carefully into the mental structure of individual patients tell us that often a psychogenic pain has a very individual meaning for the patient concerned. In one person it may derive from some great feeling of personal loss; in another from fear of abandonment. The origins may be quite idiosyncratic and sometimes extremely complex. Professor Engle in America is, however, impressed with the frequency with which psychogenic pains can ultimately be traced to feelings of guilt and the need to be punished. He talks about the "pain-prone personality" in some of his patients—a complex psychic structure in which pain is used as a way of keeping the psychological balance sheet even, as it were. In these people pain has come to perform an important function in warding off even more unpleasant feeling states. As we have already seen, pain is closely associated with comfort, aggression, punishment, and guilt, from early in development. In so far as it relieves guilt it may in some people get strongly linked to mechanisms which the mind uses to relieve guilt. Professor Engle finds that in his "pain-prone" patients their earlier lives and backgrounds have often conspired to produce an ingrained sense of guilt. Rather than accept this, the mind has fastened upon pain as a means of self-punishment and atonement. He quotes other evidence that in this type of personality other devices are used to the same end—such people are often self-depreciatory, have sought out difficult situations, or submitted to relationships in which they are hurt. This they have done repeatedly without seeming to learn from experience. The psychogenic pain often appears when at last success seems to be imminent, and conversely health is at its best when life is treating them most harshly.

What I have outlined is, of course, but a small part of a very complex theory. Such matters do not find universal agreement, but I have tried to indicate the way in which Professor Engle, a very experienced clinician, has tried to explain the source of his patient's distress. There are, of course, many such theories and no one would claim that a single system of explanation could cover every case.

In conclusion, I hope I have succeeded in demonstrating that psychological factors very often aggravate pain and may even sometimes cause pain. The importance of this is that psychological factors may equally abate and even abolish pain. Pain-relieving drugs are one of our great modern blessings, but they are not the total answer to the management of people in pain. In the management of pain, as in so many other areas of helping people, we cannot hope for simple short cuts. We need to keep alive our total understanding and our whole emotional commitment to the person in our care.

2

The Theology of Suffering

Archbishop Anthony Bloom

I speak of suffering against a background of faith, in terms more of pastoral theology than a theoretical approach to pain, taking into account what God manifests concerning pain, in the becoming of man, and in the spiritual growth of man. There is the tendency nowadays to push pain and suffering out of consciousness and out of experience, whether psychological or physical, and in that respect I feel that we create more pain than we alleviate, and we act contrary to what medical science so often has taught us. One of the principles I learnt from the very first day at the medical school was that no pain should be alleviated until it has led to understanding of the illness. If someone complains of pain in his tummy, the first thing is to find out whether it is appendicitis or something else, and only then to relieve the pain, because short of this it will be impossible to trace the cause of the original suffering. This applies also, I believe (and when I say I believe it is not any act of credulity but an act of experience) to things psychological and to suffering that originates in the spiritual condition of man. Unless we first accept the pressure of pain, trace it back to its origins, and only then look at pain as something that should be removed, we shall certainly miss every possibility we have to understand its causes and therefore look at the possibilities of cure, of putting right that which is wrong. From a biblical, from a Christian, point of view the root of pain and of suffering, whether physical or moral, the root of every disharmony, lies in our severance from God. It is Godlessness, the loss of God. It is the wrong way in which we are related to him that is at the root of suffering and pain. But this as a basic statement does not allow us to resolve every single problem. Everyone suffers from the loss of God in his own peculiar way, and we cannot simply say that by relieving pain against this background of knowledge we remain secure.

We also shrink today from the fact that pain and suffering are part of our creative becoming, and not mere hampering events of our life. One grows through suffering and pain, in strength, in faith, in maturity, in a way in which one does not grow when one lives protected against all suffering. Correlatively, the standard of life, the yardstick that allows us to evaluate life, has changed, and does change continuously. I remember my father telling me on one occasion "Whether you are alive or not is of little concern; what matters is what you are prepared to live for, and eventually to die for." But this implies a courageous, a determined, attitude to life which is not made of a continuous escape from suffering, from pain, from anguish, but is built on facing life with all its richness both of suffering and of joy, with all that it will offer, in order to face and solve problems, not in order to escape from them into an artificial security. The attempt which is made nowadays continuously, by so many people, to avoid suffering at all costs leads in fact to an increase of pain, and not to freedom from pain, because the more we try to avoid it the lower our threshold of resistance, the shorter our patience, the less our courage becomes. The result is that not only do we become more and more sensitive to suffering, but also we introduce into our life a new kind of suffering, the fear of suffering, the fear of pain, which makes pain and suffering present in our lives even at those moments when it is in fact absent.

I want now to confront you with a certain number of concrete and real situations which were worked out by men and women of faith and which led to spiritual depth. If we speak of a theology of pain we need not try to find excuses for God who allows pain, but rather to find the way in which pain allows us to grow into a new awareness, into a new depth, becoming ourselves to an extent to which we otherwise could not reach.

I begin with an example which will probably shock many of you, but one which I still believe to be an expression of a true healthy attitude to pain on the part of a believing woman. When I was working for my doctorate I was engaged in the study

of acute cancers of the breast. By chance I paid a visit to a contemporary of mine who told me that she had a boil on her breast,
and for some reason I said, "Is it a boil?" It proved to be one of
those acute cancers with which I was concerned. The woman was
a very simple person, intelligent enough, but endowed with an
extraordinary integrity and simplicity of soul. To begin with she
was profoundly distressed at the thought that her two children
of five or six years of age would be left alone, bereaved and
helpless. Then in an act of faith, that is of complete trust within
the certainty which faith means, she abandoned them to God
knowing that he would do the right thing because he was the
Lord of her health and her illness, the Lord of her death as much
as he was the Lord of her life. Where pain and suffering came into
the picture in a tremendous way was during the period when
gradually, after having received in vain all the kinds of treatment
one could offer her, she began to be very ill and to lose her
strength. Not only her breast, but also the bones of her chest
were destroyed by a quickly developing cancer. She was offered
drugs and she refused them. She said that as long as she could
endure she was prepared to endure what God had given her to
endure, not thinking of God as one deprived of mercy, pitiless,
cruel, hard, but as one who could measure the degree of pain
he would allow to the degree of courage and endurance she could
afford. When the time came, he would tell her in no uncertain
terms what was to be done next. She had an extraordinary
courage and endurance. Her bones were gradually destroyed; one
could see her lungs breathing through the wound. She suffered
indeed a great deal, not only physically but also morally. She said
"As long as I can endure I shall endure, because God can be my
strength and I can be faithful." This reminds us of the words of
St Perpetua, a martyr of North Africa, who died in the early
persecutions. She had been cast into prison a long time, being
pregnant. When the child was born she wept and moaned and one
of the soldiers in charge of the prison laughed at her and said,
"How can you expect not to give way to torture if you are in such
a state for the natural birth of a child?" And the woman answered
"I am suffering according to the law of nature. When I suffer
martyrdom it will be to God who will be my strength." This
woman took the same line. She yielded to nothing that could be
said either by her doctor or her surroundings.

Bff

One night she said to her husband, "You can now give me something to alleviate my pain. I have seen Christ standing at the foot of my bed, and something has happened to me so that now it is indifferent whether I live or die, whether I suffer or not, because in both cases God is with me." She grew into an extraordinary maturity of faith and simplicity. In that same period she felt she could no longer pray. In the past she had read morning and evening prayers. When the effort became too much her husband read them for her. The moment came when she could no longer concentrate on these prayers. It was then that she had this vision of Christ. She said to her husband, "How foolish I was ever to worry about the way I pray and the way I believe. All our faith falls into two words, 'Christos anesti', 'Christ is risen', and all prayers fall into two words 'Kyrie eleison', 'Lord, have mercy'."

This may not sound a theological approach to a theological problem, but it is theological in the sense that it is a situation in the divine context, of a person who believed without reservations, who believed heroically, who believed not only in word or in theoretical thought, but existentially. She believed in her body that Christ was the Lord of life and death, that Christ was the Lord of strength and sickness, that Christ was with her and that now, whether she died, whether she lived, it was Christ. She eventually died, having surrendered perfectly, both in body and soul, her anguish for her husband and her children as well as her bodily torment, into the hands of God.

It seems to me that this kind of answer to the problem of physical pain and moral anguish is more essential than any attempt at proving that suffering is good or wise. Here is a person who was a witness to the fact.

I would like here to make a distinction between surrender and resignation. Resignation means "to sign off", to resign from a function. Surrender means such an act of trust and confidence that you can put yourself unreservedly, joyfully, by an act of freedom, into the hand of God, whatever happens, because you are sure of him, more than you are sure of anything else. If you want a quotation, there are the words of Christ, "No one is taking my life from me, I give it freely." This is surrender, not resignation.

Now if you ask what is the place of suffering, what is the

place of anguish and pain, in the salvation of others, I would like to draw your attention to two or three examples. First of all, I remind you briefly of suffering and pain as expressed in two places, the Mount of Olives and Calvary. The anguish of Christ, before his coming death, and against a background of his vision of mankind whom he had come to save, was such that his sweat was blood. The anguish of Christ dying on the cross was such that he cried out the most tragic words in human history, "My God, my God, why hast thou forsaken me?" We can now, if not measure, at least understand more and more precisely the pain of death borne by Christ in his human nature in the crucifixion. We know now in so many ways what suffering does to a human body and how suffering affects the total human personality. But I want to put against this background of Christ, suffering in the garden of Gethsemane and dying on the cross for the salvation of mankind, what human suffering can do for men when it is accepted both in body and soul existentially and theologically. The examples which I wish to give are taken not from ancient days but from our modern contemporary history.

I would like to preface my examples with one quotation and one remark. The quotation is taken from a book by a Roman Catholic Jesuit, Cardinal Jean Danièlou, called *Holy Pagans*. He says, "Suffering is the only meeting-point between good and evil." Now if there were only good and evil and they never met, there would be the wide slippery road to hell and the narrow path to heaven. There would be no communication, no meeting-point, no way in which one can be changed into the other, or rather, perhaps, there would be no way in which a person could move from the one into the other. Hatred, cruelty, always cut into the flesh and into the soul of man, and the point at which they cut into the soul and into the body is suffering. A word that kills, a word that wounds, a blow, an act of moral or physical cruelty, does not only confront the one who is cruel with the one who is innocent, or perhaps the partly responsible sufferer. It is not a simple confrontation. The two destinies are interlocked by the events of suffering, because the two persons who have met in the act of inflicting and receiving suffering can no longer be disentangled and separated from one another in the judgement of God. The one is correlative with the other. The one who inflicted suffering will be judged because of the other, and the one who received suffering will be judged against a background of what he has received and the way in which he has taken it from his tormenter. The one remark which I want to make is that it is not the shedding of blood, the physical or moral suffering, that makes the martyr, but the survival and indeed the victory of love. You remember St Paul's hymn of love in 1 Corinthians: I will illustrate it by two examples.

In the early days of the Russian revolution a young priest was arrested and brought to trial for preaching the gospel in what has now become Leningrad. He suffered interrogation and violence. He was kept in prison for a long time. When he came out, this young man, still in his twenties, appeared an old, broken, grey-haired priest. Those who were close to him received him at the gates of the prison, looked at him, and one of them exclaimed, "What is left of you?" His answer was, "Suffering has burnt out everything. Only one thing has survived: it is love." Once out of prison he began again to preach the gospel of love that had cost him his youth, his health, his freedom, until in the end this gospel of love cost him his life in a concentration camp. Love had conquered.

I once met a priest who had spent twenty-five years in concentration camps. When we met he was a man absolutely broken in body and nerves. A noise like the snap of fingers was enough to make him jump, because twenty-five years of suffering had taught him that everything may spell suffering and pain. His physical body and nerves were beyond control, yet in an unaccountable way, at least unaccountable to me, within him there was serenity and a shining life. It was as though the soul of the man had broken its connection with that intermediary situation in which the one affects the other. It was as though the soul of this man was alive, rooted in God, shining with the divine presence, serene, unaffected by the perplexities, doubts, uncertainties, and fears, while his body was beyond control and reacted in a sort of automatic way to sound, to words, to gestures.

I offer you a few illustrations of the way in which the one who is the victim of cruelty and suffers in soul and body may yet play his part in the salvation of those who surround him. I shall not concentrate on those people who can learn from such examples, for this would be too simple and too obvious. Patience can be taught when we see the greatness of it and the fruit it bears.

Courage can be emulated, love can be received, in a heart capable of love. I am going to speak now of those people who are not receptive; who are not involved in the mystery of compassion and solidarity with the sufferer.

The first example is a man whom I was privileged to know for many years, who died recently. During the war he was arrested and sent to a concentration camp. He stayed four years in it, and when he came back I met him in one of the streets of Paris. After a few words had been exchanged, I asked him the same question that the parents and relatives had asked from the young priest mentioned before. "What have you brought back? What is left of you?" His answer was, "I have lost my peace." It gave me a shock: I expected not the loss of something but the gaining of something. I said, "Do you mean that you lost your faith?" He said, "No, but I have come back with anguish in my heart." Then he went on to explain what his anguish was about. While a prisoner in the concentration camp, submitted to all the hard and cruel conditions of the camp, suffering continually from the brutality of the system, step by step, hour after hour, meeting after meeting, in pain and anguish, he could yet say "Lord, forgive; they do not know what they do." He could, from early morning to the moment he went to sleep, forgive every act of injustice and cruelty he had to endure. He said, "While it was so, I felt I could intercede before God for the salvation of these men, because at every moment my words were 'I forgive, Lord, forgive them because they do not know what they are doing!' These words, supported by the evidence of actual suffering, gave me a right to ask God for their forgiveness." He then went on to say, "Suffering is over, but I know that one day they will stand before God's seat of judgement and be answerable for all that they have done. I pray for them, but I can give no evidence any more to God that my prayer is true, for it is not tested. What if God says on the day of judgement that these were mere words, that only those prayers which were spoken in agony of body and soul in the camp are acceptable to him?"

Well, this is a way in which moral suffering, anguish of body and soul, can be related indeed to the salvation of others, not only of those who are prepared to receive it, who long for it, but also for those who are not yet prepared to receive it. They can pass no judgement about anyone until he stands before

God and can see in the light of divine love what hatred was on earth.

Another example is also taken from the concentration camps. They are so rich in examples of utmost courage and greatness. There was published soon after the war in one of the newspapers of southern Germany a prayer found in a concentration camp written on a torn piece of wrapping paper. It was written by a man who died, and the bit of paper was kept by one of his neighbours. I cannot remember every word of it, but the essence of it is this: "O Lord, when I shall come with glory in your kingdom, do not remember only the men of goodwill. Remember also the men of evil. May they be remembered not for their acts of cruelty, the acts of evil they have done on earth, but set against their cruelty the fruits which we have borne under the stress and in the pain: the comradeship, the courage, the greatness of heart, the humility, which was born in our hearts and became part of our lives, because we suffered at their hands. May the memory of us not be a nightmare for them when they stand in judgement. May all that we have suffered be acceptable to thee as a ransom for them." This is no theoretical theology. This is not a way of trying to get God out of responsibility. These are men of blood and flesh, tested to the point of actual death, witnessing to the fact that within their incredible sufferings they proved able not only to work their own salvation but also to think of the salvation of others and indeed to work for the salvation of others.

Another example concerns one of our Russian bishops who in the course of the Stalin purges died a cruel death. Before he died he left to someone a little note in which he said: "Remember that it is given us Christians not only to believe in Christ but also to suffer for him and with him," and he added, "It is a privilege for a Christian to die a martyr, because on the day of judgement the martyrs shall be able to take their stand before the judgement seat of Christ in defence of their persecutors and say, according to their Lord's command, 'following thy example we have forgiven, thou hast no claim against these men any more'."

This is not theoretical theology. This is not an attempt at proving God right, even when he is apparently wrong. This is a witness of men who saw that he was right, within their suffering of soul and body. If that was not true, the Church would be one of the most revolting bodies one could ever imagine in the celebration of the Eucharist. The Eucharist means thanksgiving. How can a body of people, who believe in love, who believe in God, and yet see what we see around us, "thank God for all his benefits whether known or unknown" (which are words from our Orthodox liturgy). How can we thank in the face of what is going on in the world? I believe we can, but only if we can see things already fulfilled, not in imagination but in an experienced vision of the victory of God, of the light unconquered by darkness. You will remember the words of the martyrs, "Thou wert right, O Lord, in all thy ways." This is what sufferers will say at the end of time. This is what the Church, the Body of Christ, broken throughout history for the salvation of the world, not for its members only, can say now, because we know him, in whom all things have been shown us in the Garden, on the Mount of Olives, on the cross of Calvary; through whom and within whom we can see all things fulfilled through (and not only despite) suffering, through pain, hatred, and cruelty.

A thing that has struck me in the course of life in general, and perhaps more particularly in hospital work and during the war, is that people may be extraordinarily weak and yielding in the face of small suffering and tragedy, and yet become strong and steadfast in the face of things that are great. I remember a person who showed wonderful courage during the bombings of a certain city, whom I found sitting in terror on the kitchen table, between two bombings, because she had discovered a mouse! Well, this is exactly what I mean, however childish the example may be. The first thing that one must do (whether a believer or not, because a believer also needs help and support) is to believe, in the theological sense of believing; to have faith in man, in the fullness of human dignity and human greatness in him or her who suffers. We are not to destroy his courage or his strength by disbelieving that he has the greatness of man, the dignity of man, the powers of man, to stand before adversity. This is a person. That implies that we must treat people with the same reverence, with the same thoughtfulness and worship which God shows to people, that we must not let great things fritter away in small bits which we offer to their experience of suffering, so that they can never rise to their true stature and so break down continuously under the smaller things. I do not mean by this that

you must walk up to everyone and say, "You are a dying man."
What I do mean is that one should not make a man or woman who
is in danger of death a prisoner in a cobweb of lies that unnerve
him and deprive him of courage and the ability to withstand. The
first thing therefore is faith in the dignity, in the greatness, in
the resilience of men. The second, to understand that a man who
is incapable of standing up to small things may rise to greater
ones. He can then be helped to discover that within suffering
there is achievement and fulfilment in store, although perhaps not
at every actual moment. It is a victory for a man to have stood up
to suffering to the utmost. It is a victory for a man to have faced
suffering. It is a victory to a man in physical pain or moral suffering to have done in a manly way what it was right to do, to have
forgiven, made his peace, taken the initiative, because when he
looks back at what was and now is, he sees himself as someone
who possesses his soul, in a way in which he did not possess it
before. The more we teach him to face up to things, the more the
person will be able to outgrow his littleness. Of course there are
occasions when people will not be able to achieve this. There is a
measure of pain and suffering in which only the power of God
can be of help, and he is as much at work in the unbeliever as in
the believer. He is therefore for the one as entirely as he is for the
other. Was he not the atheist of the world, the only true atheist
of the world, in the sense of one totally, finally, desperately
deprived of God, when he said, "My God, my God, why hast
thou forsaken me?" He can understand, and he stands by anyone
who will say these words, or simply, "There is no God, there is
no hope." He can give life now, to anyone who stands in any of
the situations in which he stood, in anguish, godlessness, loss of
life, and all human conditions.

I think we must allow for a great deal more in a human being
than his awareness, either intellectual or emotional or physical.
A human being is a total being, body, soul, and spirit, and you
will remember how St Paul speaks of the works of the flesh.
There is a great deal to be said for good theological work to be
done to recapture, in terms of the knowledge of God, a theology
of matter, because our body is filled with the food of divine grace,
as much as our soul and spirit are merged in God. But if the
divine grace, through communion of the spirit of man with the
spirit of God, does not filter down into our psychology, to our

soul and beyond this into our body, there is no resurrection; there is a realm which is corruption in us and a realm which is eternal life. If we believe in the Incarnation, that the word became flesh, that the divinity of God united itself to the physical material body of Christ and not only to his human soul, then we must really rethink the place we give to a human being, deprived of awareness, profoundly wounded in his mental, intellectual, and emotional processes. I think it is terribly important that all our Churches should rethink the problems of matter, of the Incarnation, of the sacraments, of miracles, against that kind of background, because what makes our theologies so hopelessly inadequate is that we all, implicitly or explicitly, accept the material world on the terms of the materialist and, having accepted the material world in that way, we then put on top of it, or push into it, things like incarnation, the change of bread and wine into the body and blood of Christ, the miracles, and so on. We then have to work out two kinds of theology. It is either a magic theology, or a theology that makes nonsense of what we say. When we say, for instance, "in a spiritual manner", we usually mean "I don't believe it, but I say it": because we do not make friends "in a spiritual manner"; we do not eat our lunch "in a spiritual manner". We do things "in a spiritual manner" only when we want to keep the word safe from our complete disbelief in the event. We will never solve this problem unless we have an adequate theology of things material, and then we can as doctors, nurses, chaplains, and so on, think of the bodies of people whom we treat in quite new terms, in terms that begin with the seed sown in corruption and ending with the transfiguration and the ascension and the sitting at the right hand of the Father.

Some years ago I had occasion to speak about suffering on television with Malcolm Muggeridge. I later received two letters on the same day, the one from a very passionate and ferocious gentleman who on four big pages told me that I knew nothing of suffering, that I had never suffered myself and therefore spoke with arrogance and lack of understanding. By the same post there was another letter, signed by a group of survivors from the camp at Buchenwald, saying that what I had said in the broadcast, which basically I have tried to convey to you, was true from within their experience and made sense intellectually of what certain of them had experienced and not put into words. So before you dismiss this existential suffering and pain which I have tried to convey to you by examples, think of their witness and ask yourselves whether you have another testimony to bring, not the testimony of your doubt, but the testimony of your experience, of your bodies and of your souls.

3

The Psychology of the Dying

John Hinton

The people we are to consider are those who have an illness which will, before long, bring about their death. Although our attention may immediately be captured by the fact that the person is going to die, the concern of many patients is liable to be focused on the quality of life they are experiencing during their terminal illness. Because the dying and their relatives and friends may be as troubled about the problems of existence as of dying, it is appropriate to discuss first of all the obvious changes brought about by the incurable illness.

SYMPTOMS

Disease, especially terminal disease, is often associated in people's minds with pain. Fatal illness is by no means bound to cause pain. It may do, but one can reasonably expect nowadays to be relieved of intolerable pain fairly promptly and in terminal conditions pain should be kept under control. Some patients, rightly or wrongly, do not feel certain enough of their care and anticipate days of physical discomfort. They are likely to be apprehensive or fearful of this prospect and some, unfortunately, may still experience considerable pain interrupted by periods of relief which are marred by the expectation that the discomfort will return. In these circumstances people cannot steadily prepare themselves for the end of their life, although they may impulsively, and to some extent justifiably, wish the end would come. Their mental outlook is likely to be limited by their discomfort rather than making a calm readjustment to their changing situation. Some individuals show great fortitude in their suffering, and some may add a positive quality to their character after times of endurance, but for many useless distress means a loss of dignity and morale.

Pain is not the only symptom which can trouble a person and threaten to make miserable his remaining days. There are symptoms with which many of you who visit and care for the sick must be familiar. Nausea, vomiting, persistent coughing, and exhaustion may prove very troublesome to some individuals and these symptoms cannot always be relieved completely. Patients are then liable to regard their existence as a series of bad or not so bad days according to the degree of their discomfort. They may become understandably preoccupied by the search for treatment which will bring relief. If relief does not come, then they are liable to become worn down and depressed.

Certain physical symptoms are likely to cause particular emotional reactions. It is probable that most people will have empathy for those who cannot breathe properly and are prone to become anxious or have moments of panic. People who lose control over their bladder or bowels may become very upset over their incontinence. Those who have been particular about their hygiene and scrupulous over attention to detail may well suffer agonies at this loss of control, blaming themselves for their filthy state and resentful at the necessity of depending on others. A sense of deep shame may be brought about by quite a few symptoms produced by fatal conditions. Some people still regard cancer itself as a thing to be ashamed of. Others are embarrassed by visible tumours or bodily mutilations consequent upon disease or necessary operations. If a woman loses her hair following radiotherapy to the head, or if a person emits a smell because of a colostomy or a discharging lesion, they may be very troubled in the company of others. Disabilities of speech, paralyses, gross wasting, can all depress morale so the quality of life is sadly impaired.

Most people do not endure extreme discomfort nor long periods of distress during their final illness. In part this is due to the nature of some fatal conditions which do not necessarily cause great physical suffering. In part the absence of distress is due to the efficacy of well-judged palliative care which can make all the difference to the quality of life even if it cannot prolong it greatly. When distressing symptoms are uncontrolled they are likely to assume primary importance. Other matters appear subsidiary unless they help to relieve distress or at least distract attention for a while. For those not preoccupied by the presence or imminence of discomfort, there are other matters to heed.

CONSEQUENCES OF ILLNESS

Many aspects of life are seen in a different perspective when one changes from being an ordinary person to being a patient. It can sometimes appear that the role of the patient has its attractions. One can become the recipient of care instead of being caught up with the feverish activity of everyday life which often appears to achieve very little. There will be relaxation in bed instead of bustle. Some classic writing may be read instead of being by-passed; responsibilities will be surrendered to others; pleasant, enjoyable trivia will replace the important-sounding demands which too often clamour for attention. There will be time to think, to meditate, to plan, and to dream.

All these things may and do occur for some people in their terminal illness, for example, the elderly person who considers that his life has been satisfying. He can exchange work and responsibilities for a passive role while the next one or two generations take their turn. But many people find it difficult to surrender former activities and responsibilities which may even have seemed to be their justification for living. They regret the loss of strength and their former power of doing things without a second thought. During the illness their abilities may have declined from coping with a responsible, demanding occupation, to a less important job and absences from work, to half-pay and tentative hopes for a return to their job, and finally to a bed-ridden existence. Not many housewives can feel at ease when they become enforced invalids and their aged husband or visiting children take over and carry out the household tasks in a slightly different way.

The seriously ill may well grieve over their loss of abilities, their altered appearance, the loss of their former role in life, or their diminishing independence. Such a loss can bring about the classic response to loss, that is, depression. As with other losses, however, sadness is not the only reaction. There can be irritability or outright anger at the enforced surrender of control. The necessity to depend on others produces not only gratitude and passivity but also resentment and criticism. Grown men and women may well react to the limitations imposed by illness in ways reminiscent of the frustrated child. Even when they are aware of their childlike responses they may repeatedly try to do things which are now outside the range of their abilities or make demands for attention or even indulge in tantrums. This is in spite of a logical appreciation of the situation or the knowledge that they will subsequently feel ashamed at their behaviour. Such reactions may demand easy tolerance from those who look after the sick; it does not, incidentally, imply that the sick need to be treated as children.

Being ill is also good cause for anxiety. Uncertainty about day-to-day developments or the eventual prognosis may give rise to worry. There may be apprehension about going to hospital, or fears about the burden imposed on relatives if they stay at home. There is no need to list the concerns of those admitted or re-admitted to hospital. Patients may be very appreciative of the care they get there which cannot be obtained elsewhere, but it can be very disturbing to be uprooted from familiar places and people and thrust into the strange, sometimes threatening hospital world. Other worries come with serious illness and insurance can only guard against a few of them. Financial problems or, at least, a drop in the standard of living may prove very worrying to people who consider it their job to earn enough for the family needs. Women may be very troubled if they fear they can no longer look after their family or their homes properly. There can be fears about treatment or about not having treatment; anxieties over being lonely and insecure; concern over relatives and—do not underrate it—over pets; worries about what will happen if someone knocks at the door or if the district nurse will fail to come. And amongst these anxieties, and sometimes at the root of displaced fears, is concern about the outcome of the disease. Will I get better?

AWARENESS OF DYING

When people have an illness likely to prove fatal there will soon be evidence for them to suspect the nature of their condition.

They may well reject their early suspicions because they are not prepared to entertain such thoughts. They may be "unprepared" in more than one sense, being both unwilling and also unready to receive the knowledge. People may also disregard the serious prognostic significance of the progress of the illness because others assure them that they will get better.

What sort of evidence does come unsought to people to indicate to them that their condition is irrecoverable? The character of the illness may be revealing—serious symptoms which obviously threaten existence such as gross breathlessness which does not respond to treatment or tumours which get progressively larger or crop up all over the place. It is the progress of the condition which often carries a solemn message; if there is an improvement in one disorder another two symptoms seem to replace it. Many of the symptoms of terminal disease eventually seem to be there to stay, perhaps being controlled but not cured by treatment. The condition may fluctuate, but the overall progress is downhill.

Many of the clues come not from the illness but from other people who know or suspect the diagnosis or even from the nature of the treatment administered. It is only too easy for doctors, nurses, and others caring for the sick to forget the fact that although ill people may become very dependent on them for treatment and skill they do not necessarily suspend all their critical powers. Some patients may choose, unconsciously or consciously, to surrender all responsibility to a nurse or doctor, but others may well feel almost the opposite. Any of you who have been patients wishing to know what the hospital staff have learnt from investigations or what relatives have been told, will realize how watchfulness will reveal at least partial truth, even if the spoken words are not meant to carry the message. A single consummate actor may be able to deceive a dying patient for a long while, but the varying attitudes and hesitations when several are involved soon indicate that something serious is afoot if—and it is worth repeating the if—the patient is prepared to recognize it. The professional optimism may slip if the patient asks too pointed a question about the future. A patient in a hospital ward may catch a glimpse of some negative facial expression or overhear a discussion on a report which may hint at deeper aspects to the reassurance received. The nature of the operation or radiotherapy may show that the lesion was far from trifling. Other patients in a ward may be only too willing to share their knowledge or opinions of various illnesses even if the staff are not. If a relative has been told that the condition is likely to be fatal and tries to keep this knowledge from the patient, there is often an area of restraint which communicates the unease about the situation.

With these and many other straws in the wind it is probable that the majority of people have some recognition of the serious nature of their fatal illness. The easier the communication that exists with the dying the greater the proportion who acknowledge that they may not have long to live. This is not just because less inhibited talk results in many patients being told they will not recover—such frankness is not the rule in Britain today and few will offer gratuitous information to patients that the illness will prove fatal. Yet a half or more of people who are in hospital during their terminal illness are prepared to indicate or talk forthrightly—given the chance—about their views that the outcome may be a fatal one. On the whole, awareness grows as life gets nearer to the end, but this is a generalization which misses out an important aspect of the situation—that is, the fluctuation in views expressed by dying individuals. Sometimes they wish to concentrate their thoughts on hopes of recovery, sometimes there is greater acknowledgement of life coming to an end. To some people they may wish to express faith in recovery, with others they share their doubts or their more sombre views. Moreover, while some people do not want to hear a patient's anxieties or pertinent comments about dying, others can receive such views.

SPEAKING OF DYING

This last-mentioned aspect of people's awareness of dying emphasizes that it is unrealistic to consider their awareness or attitude to dying without taking into account the feelings of the people around them. The views of those close to the dying may well be at least equally mixed, equally ambivalent, as the patient's. Even if it is not their own life which is ending they may feel a responsibility for helping the patient. It can also happen that the people at the bedside are more troubled at the prospect of bereavement than the dying person is disturbed by thoughts of death.

When people's views have been sought on the question of being told about having a fatal illness, the very large majority, about four out of five, say that they would like to be told. Rather fewer believe that others should be told—they seem less sure about the quality of other people's characters than their protested confidence in their own stability. When it comes to asking the views of the people who would be in the position of having to tell people that they are not going to recover, considerably fewer people are emphatic that this is the right policy. This is not simple cowardice, for the same people—usually doctors—are prepared to tell the closest relative. That is no easy task, but most are convinced that it is the right thing to do. Not nearly so many believe in telling a person openly that he may soon cease to exist.

There are, of course, other factors which come into the situation. The doctors who wish to cure, and think it best that their patients have faith in their ability to cure, may not be able to cope easily with the situation when they are failing in this respect. It is not just that they may feel impotent or lose some self-respect, but they fear that telling a person that his illness is likely to end in his death may destroy the patient's morale. They feel they just "can't". Anyone who has been in this situation must feel some sympathy with this viewpoint. There is a sense of confirming a sentence and a feeling that one may be destroying much-needed hope. In addition, to commit everyone to an open acknowledgement that there will be no recovery tends to destroy many of the touches of unrealistic optimism which people like to bring into the conversation at the bedside.

The frequent policy which does evolve in conversations between the dying and those around him is a tacit collusion to deny that he is going to die. If this game is played expertly, as it so often is by the patient and his attendants without anyone needing to explain the rules, it can be comforting to all concerned. They can reassure each other that it is going to be all right. If one of the team shows signs of not playing his part and shows doubts or distress about the real outcome, another can comfort, persuade, or deny to him until he can once more be diverted and contribute to the accepted policy. Sometimes the lapse is ignored in the certainty that no one is going to persist in flouting the consensus that it will all work out for the best. Incidentally it is not always patients who need the reassurance; it is not rare for them to be comforting those who are going to live.

Unfortunately, this policy of denial is not always successful. The fears of developing progressive pain, or continued discomfort, or of not being looked after properly, or even of dying may not always be allayed by reassurance. If treatment was prescribed with bold statements about cure, failure may bring disillusion. If the patient has recognized in himself that he may be dying and wants to speak a little more realistically about this even for just a while, he can feel very isolated if no one listens. He may want to do no more than voice a doubt qualified by many ifs and buts; to be met by nothing but bland optimism from all around him is likely to cause increasing anxiety which will destroy the usefulness of maintaining the masquerade. The visitors who rely on the façade of optimism and cannot manage without it may reduce their visits or their real communication to a minimum if they become embarrassed by the patient's progress to death. In these uncomfortable situations the dying person may feel he is having to come to terms with death without help from others. Some may prefer it this way, but others would like help because they do not find it an easy thing to bear alone.

FEAR AND SADNESS WHEN DYING

For many people thought of death and dying are fearful. Death has become associated in our minds with so many frightening things. Not all aspects of death are feared. Some people have found solace in the fact that death means a rest from worldly struggles. Others have seen the need for a finite end to existence in order to give greater meaning and pleasure to the enjoyment of living. Death, for the majority of those who are inspired by Christian faith, must also mean the threshold of new life. In spite of such comforts, however, death also carries with it connotations of destruction, ruin, decay, anarchy, chaos, loss of control, grief, suffering, and punishment. If death were to mean just these last-mentioned things, then dying would indeed be a fearful time.

It is clear that dying can be a time of anxiety but, given a reasonable standard of care, fear does not predominate in the way that many people anticipate. Much of the anxiety that does exist is in connection with some of the factors mentioned before—the fear of suffering, and anxiety over others. This last anxiety can be considerable when death is coming to younger people who feel with justification that their children or other relatives will suffer hardship from their loss. There may also be considerable anxiety when people are unsure whether they are likely to live or die—the complete uncertainty may be less bearable than resignation sprinkled with hopes.

The fear of death itself does not usually give rise to so much alarm in those who are actually dying. They may be distressed for a few days as they come to terms with the idea, but usually this particular anxiety does not continue to cause distress. It would be unrealistic to expect people not to show any apprehension at the fact that their life is coming to an end. In many ways, however, it is remarkable that so many people rarely show anything but cheerfulness and courage, and most others soon regain their composure after some upset at the enormous change in the quality of their circumstances.

The unpleasant mood that the dying experience is more likely to be sadness rather than fear. If people recognize that they are probably approaching death and yet they do not really wish to die yet, then there is sorrow. As mentioned before, a sense of loss brings depression and dying people face many losses. They stand to lose their independence and their customary position in life; they may well be separated from their friends and relatives; their change in health may prevent them from doing the things they enjoyed and they are faced with the loss of existence itself. Once again, in fact, given company, affection, and help most people come to terms with this also. If there is persistent physical discomfort and spiritual isolation, however, it is likely that depression will continue to cause mental suffering.

WAYS OF FACING DEATH

How can people come to terms with a knowledge that is potentially distressing to them. One common way of coping has already been mentioned—the mind pretends that the possibility does not exist. People can do this fairly consciously. They are fleetingly aware in the back of their mind what the real situation is. Then they never allow themselves to consider the matter further, lest they suffer. This sort of process is not necessarily done consciously. When people are faced with overwhelming emotions, these feelings and the knowledge of the cause can be banished entirely from the conscious mind. The dying person who denies all knowledge of this state may never appreciate that the knowledge is locked away in his mind. If very effectively repressed it should cause no mental pain, but sometimes a sense of anxiety remains.

Another way of coping is to fight against the disease, refuse to surrender to fate. Many people show great courage in their determination to get better. They make light of their symptoms and force themselves to do as much as they can. When they talk of their disease they are more likely to speak of the latest optimistic sign or the most recent achievement, such as, "I walked round the bed yesterday", or they may voice their immediate hopes. "Doctor's just started me on some new tablets" or "I may visit home next weekend". In one way it is easy to collude with such patients, especially as their determination seems so admirable. Problems arise when they seek or demand treatments which have minimal chances of improving their condition and may, in fact, cause discomfort or greater disability. They may feel fobbed off if those who care for them do not seem to have the same enthusiasm for cure as they do themselves. Very often the relatives who are fighting hard to deny that the patient is going to die may be even more insistent that no stone is left unturned.

Such feelings introduce the issue that not all the emotions involved in dying have a positive or sympathetic quality. When people feel that they may well die—or lose someone dear to them—resentment and jealousy may arise. If people very much want to live and yet it appears that life is being taken from them, then it is understandable for them to blame someone or something. It is unlikely that doctors or anyone else around the dying have behaved perfectly during the development and progress of the last illness and so it is not difficult for the dying to find some human targets to blame and criticize. The inability to cure is an important enough failure. If the patients do not blame people, they may still feel that there is an injustice in their situation. It is easy for them to envy the good health of others and to resent the fact that they themselves are ill while others have kept their strength and their prospects of living.

The problems of the dependency of patients on others also link up with this. It is not always easy for people to be entirely grateful to those who are helping and caring for them. The loss of independence may be felt very keenly. Each caring act is a reminder of helplessness and each failure of the others to provide the exact help needed emphasizes even more their own subordination. This can give rise to patients being very troubled by their mixed feelings of gratitude and irritability. Usually they try to suppress the irritation and anger they feel but it can erupt and trouble all concerned—not least the person who has felt and shown his anger. It is not always people who are blamed. Although many people strengthen their faith in God when they are mortally ill, a few will feel that God has let them down. Their prayers and desires seem to meet no response and they may turn away.

A great many people, however, meet the end of their life with acceptance. They often say so. Their awareness of their condition increases step by step with their increasing ability to acknowledge the situation. There are changes in attitudes; the striving and the clinging to hopes become less necessary. Aspects of work and life which previously appeared so important may now be viewed as irrelevant. There is a recognition that the active phase of life is over. Many people wish to do a bit of tidying up of their lives at this point; put affairs in order or straighten out relationships which have become entangled or neglected for some while.

If physical discomfort is controlled, with care and companionship the end of life can be pleasant. When it is recognized, either openly or tacitly, by the patient that he does not have long to live, it does not mean that the remaining part of his life is not important. Occasionally, by the way, dying people feel that others appear a bit too expeditious about their departure. If illness has not blurred the quality of life too much, the last phase of life in this world can be very precious. People can and do accept with dignity that they are dying. It tends to come more easily to those who have completed their expected life span. They still need care and suitable encouragement. Many people who know they are dying will still speak of hopes—either of improvement or tentative future plans. Their conversation often holds the implication that they will not suffer disillusion and disappointment if these voiced hopes do not materialize, but they like to toy with them.

For many people the end of their life is given a further meaning through their religion. They gain their support and their hope through their faith. This is reinforced if those responsible for their religious care have the personal qualities of understanding for which many dying people have expressed their appreciation.

4

The Psychology of Bereavement

C. Murray Parkes

I speak as a psychiatrist who has worked for some years trying to understand the problem of bereavement—how people cope with it, viewing it as a stress or a major change in their lives. The fact that I am a psychiatrist of course gives me a bias. Doctors tend to treat the sick, psychiatrists the mentally sick, and there is a tendency to assume that because the psychiatrist is talking about bereavement therefore bereavement must lead to some dreadful consequences for the personality and the lives of people who undergo it. I would like to state at the outset that I do not think this is necessarily the case. It is true that bereavement may be a time of life when people can develop both physical and mental illnesses, but it is also a time when they may cultivate a new maturity, a new strength. In focusing therefore on the difficulties I would not wish to create the impression that they are either inevitable or insurmountable. Most of my own work has been with newly bereaved men and women; women losing husbands and men losing wives.

The word that comes to mind when one is talking about bereavement is "grief". Grief is the reaction to a major loss, and of course it is a reaction to many different types of loss, bereavement being only one of them. What follows will therefore have some applicability outside the field of bereavement.

Grief, as reaction to loss, is not the only thing that follows bereavement. Other things have to be taken into account if we are to understand the behaviour of bereaved people. If grief is the reaction to loss, deprivation is the reaction to unmet needs. A woman whose husband has died not only loses her husband, but she has to go through life without her spouse, without his companionship, without many of the financial possessions that she has lost with him. Clearly her reaction to bereavement will be coloured by the loneliness which arises from the loss of companionship and by the problems that arise as a result of bereavement in terms of home, money, etc. She also has to undergo a major change in role. She is no longer a married woman; she is a widow, and in every culture widows are treated in a different way from married women, and different expectations obtain.

In addition to being a widow the bereaved person may also see herself as a survivor. This "survivor role" is one which was not recognized by psychologists until the calamities of World War II. Attention was drawn to the fact that where a major disaster had occurred, those who survived were very special people. For example, those who survived concentration camps often carried a load of what has been called "survival guilt". Of course people deal with their guilt in different ways, but there is a tendency for some to blame themselves for the fact of having survived; in some way to identify with the dead and to feel that they themselves ought to be dead. In Hiroshima, according to Robert Lifton, some of the people who survived the bomb even now, 25 years later, are still waiting to die, and sit around aimlessly with little or no will to live. These people's lives seem to have ended at the time of the disaster. To a lesser extent, anyone who has survived a major bereavement may in some sense be tied to the past. They may feel guilty at having survived, and have somehow taken on the role of waiting for death, giving up their investment in an ongoing life.

Mention must also be made of the reaction of society to the widowed, for in many cultures she is placed under the most strict taboos. In this country we like to think we are free from such superstitions and that we do not stigmatize our bereaved. Sadly, there is evidence that as a nation we do. Many widows to whom I have talked have said that in bereavement "you find out who your friends are". By this they usually mean that there are certain people they may have known very well who just don't come to visit them any more. They find that some people react to them with embarrassment and fear, and seem unable to communicate with them as ordinary human beings. With bereavement there comes a loss of status, for there is a tendency to pity the bereaved, and pity in itself can be demeaning. In this respect it is worth while drawing a distinction between pity and sympathy. This was pointed out by Phyllis Calvert when she described her experience as a widow. Sympathy involves sharing something. It is having someone who is somehow able to get close enough to you to share your grief, to share something of the awareness of the situation. It is a very different thing from the experience of pity, which only puts you at a greater distance from the person who is pitying you.

I turn now to look more closely at grief itself, and shall describe some of the results of interviewing at three-monthly intervals twenty-two widows during their first year of bereavement. They were women to whom I was first introduced by general practitioners who had agreed to help me with this study. Practically all of the people I interviewed were anxious to talk. In fact, these interviews lasted for anything up to three or four hours, and they seemed to give the widows an opportunity to talk about a whole set of fears and anxieties which were preoccupying them. They would often confess, "There is nobody else I can talk to in this way." I was very much struck at that time by the fact that I found myself performing a role which is traditionally performed by the clergy. Visiting the bereaved is something which has been regarded as an important part of the role of the clergy, and they too have the opportunity of allowing and helping people to talk through their problems as these women talked through their problems with me. What I was concerned to do was to try to get a picture from them of the husband's illness, how they reacted to it, what their experience had been since, and what they saw as some of the things that had helped and/or hindered them since that time. On this basis they were all very cooperative.

Among the twenty-two widows there were nineteen who had some warning of the seriousness of their husband's condition prior to death. It is very interesting that only six of these had fully accepted what they had been told. The remainder either disbelieved the diagnosis or they believed the diagnosis but not the prognosis. They persisted in the belief that their husbands were going to go on living very much longer than had been indicated to them, and it seemed to be exceptional for them to prepare themselves fully for what was to come. Fourteen of them nursed their husbands at home. They all experienced this as a great strain, but part of the problem was that they felt they could not communicate openly with their husband about his illness. The traditional way of treating a terminally ill patient is to keep the truth about his illness from him, and the families and doctors took great pains to try and protect the dying patient from knowledge of the fact that he was dying. In these instances, when death actually occurred, the reaction was quite naturally a very severe one. The initial reaction of about half the widows was the feeling of numbness or blunting—a complete blanking out of feelings. From time to time there might be extreme outbursts of anger or despair, but most of the time they would say, "I felt nothing—I just couldn't take it in". This feeling of numbness usually lasted from a few hours to a few days; it was then followed by the onset of the pangs of grief—a period of intense pining for the lost person. Pangs of grief are very painful. They usually reach their peak within five to seven days of the bereavement, and they occur particularly when anything reminds the widow of her loss. They are associated with intense anxiety, psychological pain, dryness in the mouth, and all the signs doctors associate with acute anxiety. During this period the widow tends to be preoccupied with thoughts of her loss, restless, tense and going over in her mind again and again the events leading up to it. As one widow put it, "I never stop missing him". Another said, "I am continually searching for something to do, but I can't find what to do". They feel drawn towards places and objects associated with the dead person and possessions that remind them of him are treasured. Along with this preoccupation there is a tendency to picture the dead person very clearly and vividly. One widow exclaimed, "I can almost feel his skin and touch his hands". It is as if they carried in their minds a constant picture of the husband. From time to time they may actually think they hear or see him around. Nine of these widows described hallucinations and illusions of the presence of the husband. For instance, one woman said, "I was walking down the street and I saw my husband walking towards me, but when I got close enough I could see it wasn't him after all". Fifteen of them described a strong sense of the husband's presence nearby—they felt he was in the room, somewhere around.

What is the explanation of these feelings? The stage of pining or yearning can best be understood if we look at the way animals react to major losses. An animal separated from its young, or the young separated from the mother, begins to cry. They become restless; they search, and they lose interest in their food and other activities, becoming totally preoccupied with the problem of finding the lost object. A human being of course knows that when someone has died it is no good searching to find him again, but I think we are left nevertheless with this instinctive need to search for the person who has gone. This need expresses itself in the pining, the clear visual memories that have been described, as well as the tendency to misidentify things. We have all experienced such feelings when desperately searching for a lost object. Psychologists refer to "a perceptual set"—i.e. we are set to see a particular object, and because we are anxious to see it we tend to see it.

The pangs of grief are at first very severe. However, they decline gradually in intensity and duration, and between periods of pining the bereaved person tends to be depressed, apathetic, and somewhat disorganized. The widow sometimes makes an attempt to short-circuit grief by avoiding people who will remind her of it, and will shut herself up at home. She will often say, "I still can't believe it's true that he's gone", even a year after bereavement. Many people try to control grief by controlling their thoughts. They say, "I try to keep busy", and avoid all thoughts of grief, deliberately occupying every moment of their time so that they cannot leave themselves time to grieve.

The attitude of the newly widowed towards the world seems to change: instead of being a secure place in which they know what to do and how to do it, the world is suddenly seen to be dangerous and insecure. Some feel it more difficult to trust people. One woman said to me, "I want to get a ferocious dog that will bite the throat of any man who comes near me". It was quite clear that she felt the need to defend herself against a man. To what extent she was trying to defend herself against her own feelings, her own need for a man, in this way, is another matter, but this kind of attitude is not at all uncommon.

As time passes, the intensity and duration of the pangs of grief diminish, interests and appetites return, and among the first needs is that for food. Of the widows I talked to, practically all lost a great deal of weight during the first month of bereavement, but within three months they were well on the way to putting back their usual weight. Nevertheless it may be some time—perhaps several years—before a widow can really begin to look to the future and replan her life with any sense of pleasure. This is something which occurs gradually, and is certainly affected by things that go on around her, such as whether she gets a job or not, or whether she has a family close at hand. In other words, her ability to find new interests in life, and to look outward and forward to the future rather than inward and backward to the past, will depend to a large extent on what kind of a world she finds herself in.

People often ask, "How long does grief last?" There is no simple answer to this question. Many years may have elapsed since a bereavement, but some event, such as an anniversary, or the finding of a photograph in a drawer, may bring back quite vividly the memories of that loss. The bereaved person may go again through the process of pining and searching, albeit in a much reduced form. There is therefore no clear end-point to grief. Nevertheless it is true that grief tends to follow the kind of course that has been described, with a phase of numbness, a phase of pining and yearning, a phase of disorganization and depression, and finally a phase of reorganization and restoration of interest in life. One other factor which I think is important and needs to be mentioned is the way in which feelings of anger and guilt commonly complicate the course of grief. Two-thirds of the widows I talked to admitted to feelings of anger which they could see were quite irrational. For instance, they would seize on something their husband said, or something someone had said to their husband which hurt him in the course of his illness, and magnify this and express great anger towards the person who had said it. This seemed sometimes to be part of an attempt to search for a cause for the illness, for someone to punish. Whilst the widow may blame others for what has happened, she is equally likely to blame herself; to find some minor misdemeanour, something that she neglected to do or something she had said about which she can express feelings of guilt. These guilt feelings are particularly prominent in people who develop atypical or pathological forms of grief.

Let us, therefore, consider some of the atypical symptoms of grief. I was able to obtain access to the General Practitioners' case notes of a series of forty-four widows who had been registered with the same general practitioners for two years before and after their bereavements. It was clear from examining these case notes that these widows were visiting their general practitioners very much more frequently after the bereavement than they had beforehand. There was in fact a 240% increase in the consultation rate during the first six months after bereavement among the widows under the age of 65. Over the age of 65 there was also an increase in consultations, although not such a great one; this increase was not confined to consultations for what might be called psychiatric or psychological symptoms. In the younger age-group a large proportion of the bereaved women were going to the general practitioner for sleeping tablets or a tonic, something for their depression, as for other symptoms associated with grief. There were also a large number, particularly in the over-65 age group, who went along with a variety of physical complaints ranging from rheumatism and arthritis to indigestion and a variety of minor disturbances which were not at first glance directly related to the bereavement, or at least did not appear to be. Quite why the over-65 age group showed no increase in requests for sedatives or for help with emotional problems I do not know. There has not been a great deal of research done with older bereaved people. Certainly there is no evidence that bereavement in that age group does not cause the same kind of problems as arise among younger people. There have been studies of depressed patients in psychiatric hospitals for instance which suggest that depressions in old age can very often be caused by bereavement. It does not, however, appear from the general practitioner's point of view that depression is one of the symptoms that commonly takes an old person to her doctor—she is much more likely to go with a physical complaint.

I was able, with the help of the General Registry Office to study several thousand men whose wives died during two specific months in 1957. These widowers were followed up over a period of ten years. There was a sharp increase in mortality rate among these men during the first six months, maintained at a slightly lower level during the whole of the first year of bereavement. Furthermore, when the causes of death were examined, the majority were given as coronary thrombosis or arteriosclerotic heart disease. This group of heart disease is a very common cause of death but, when compared with the death rate one would have expected among married people, it was clear that it accounted for a much larger share of the increased mortality than any other cause of death. Perhaps there may be something in the old notion that you can die of a broken heart! Why people die from heart disease following a bereavement no one yet knows. It may be, for instance, that bereaved people smoke more, and since smoking and coronary thrombosis are related this factor may be producing an increased death rate from coronary thrombosis. More research needs to be done in order to explain this particular finding.

Another source of information about things that go wrong after bereavement is of course admissions to psychiatric hospitals. Studying patients admitted to two London psychiatric clinics, it was clear that the number of people admitted within six months of the death of husband or wife was six times greater than it would have been if the admission had been just a chance expectation and there had been no relationship between the cause of admission and the bereavement. The types of illness which these bereaved psychiatric patients had were very often depressive illnesses; but they included quite a wide variety of other complaints. For instance, people who might have been heavy drinkers all their lives are very likely, after the death of husband or wife, to drink just that much more, which may precipitate them into an alcoholic psychosis. Similarly, people with a history of neurosis or personality disorders found them recurring with greater intensity following bereavement.

In a further study I was able to interview twenty-one psychiatric patients who had all developed a mental illness within six months of the death of a close relative. In fifteen of these it was quite clear that the patient had not recovered from grief. He was still suffering from chronic grief long after the death of the loved person. Grief had continued for well over the time, and with an intensity very much greater than one would have expected. There was a minority, eight patients, who had not shown intense grief at the time of bereavement; in fact they had shown very little feeling at all during that period, and for several weeks afterwards their grief had been delayed. When eventually their grief did break through, it tended to be a much more severe and lasting form. It appeared from this and other studies that people who inhibit or fail to express grief are particularly likely to get into difficulties later. Even during the period of delay many of these people were showing some sort of symptom—perhaps having sudden unexplained panic attacks when they felt they had to rush out of a room, or having severe and unpleasant nightmares at night, or developing a rash or some psychosomatic symptom which might take them to the doctor. One other kind of pathological grief state is that in which there is a permanent inhibition of grief. This type of inhibited grief is thought to be common among bereaved children. Children who have suffered a major bereavement may not express very much grief at the time, and it may be years later before they break down. At this point they may develop psychiatric illness. There are many psychiatrists who regard it as an important form of psychotherapy to trace back psychological symptoms to a loss in early life, with the object of trying to help the person who has undergone this loss to express and work through his grief. It seems that if we do not express grief it is going to find an outlet in some other way.

Among the bereaved psychiatric patients mentioned above, feelings of guilt tended to be particularly pronounced and there had often been a bad relationship between husband and wife. This may appear somewhat strange at first, for if the one partner had not established a good relationship with the other we might expect that sorrow would be reduced to a minimum. When there is a disturbed relationship between husband and wife there is often a secret wish that the other may die. When such wishes come true the survivor feels as if he has been magically responsible. Grief, in such cases, seems to persist as an attempt to make up for the griever's own sense of guilt.

Other problems reported by these bereaved psychiatric patients included panic attacks, which were not at all uncommon, particularly at times when the wife might have come home from work. Other symptoms which were quite common (occurring five times in the twenty-one bereaved psychiatric patients) were what has been called identification symptoms. The bereaved person develops a set of symptoms very similar to those which the husband or wife suffered during the last illness. It is a hypochondriacal illness which repeats the illness of the person who has died. For instance, one man I talked to worked in his father's firm. He clearly modelled himself on his father. When his father died the son developed a pain in his chest which caused the doctor to have him admitted to hospital with a diagnosis of coronary thrombosis. Once he could see the link between his father's and his own symptoms the son got better.

Another illustration of this kind of thing occurred in a patient whom I was treating in psychotherapy when her father died. Right after his death she had a dream, in which she saw him lying in his coffin. He reached out of his coffin and stroked the right side of her body, whereupon she woke up and found that the right side of her body was paralysed. Her father had died from a "stroke" affecting the right side of his body.

Why is it that some people get into these difficulties while others do not? There are three main factors to be borne in mind. First of all, there are features influencing the magnitude and the nature of the grief itself. You might expect, for instance, a chronic grief reaction to occur when a husband or wife has been highly dependent on the person who has died, and has lived in one of those symbiotic relationships where each of them almost lives through the other. One such widow described her reaction by saying: "I feel as though half of myself has died".

A further factor influencing the magnitude of grief itself is the mode of death. Sudden unexpected losses seem to give rise to more prolonged and severe reactions than losses for which a person has had time to prepare. Road accidents or sudden disasters often give rise to such reactions.

Yet another group of factors which determine how people react to bereavement is the question of defence—how people defend themselves against their own grief. Many people attach a great deal of importance to not showing feelings or breaking down. This is not just a matter of personal idiosyncrasy. There is a tendency, which is greater in our western culture today than perhaps it has ever been in any other culture, to hide feelings; to "keep a stiff upper lip"; to attach great value to the control of the emotions. People who have this need may very well develop difficulties in the grief situation. I remember talking to one young American whose wife had died. He did not cry at all after his wife's death until, at the funeral, he saw his father cry. He said this was a terrible shock to him, because he had never seen his father cry before: he did not think his father would ever be so weak. And yet, when his father cried, this somehow gave him permission to cry. He felt for the very first time that he was in a situation where it was actually permissible for him to cry.

The other group of factors which tend to affect the nature of grief are those which arise in the home and its environment. Difficulties often arise when the bereaved person is socially isolated, when the children are married and have left home. In such circumstances the widow may shut herself up at home. She may not want to meet people for a time because of the fact that they remind her of what has happened, so she severs the links with people around her who might be able to help. Eventually they forget about her, and after a while nobody comes round any more.

Just occasionally the opposite situation arises, where the family remain at home but perpetuate grief by expecting mother to go on mourning for father for ever. Queen Victoria is the classic example of the chronic grief reaction. Perhaps because of her position, perhaps because she had an image of herself as being royal and therefore bigger than anybody else, her grief had to be greater than that of other people. Her love for Prince Albert was expressed in terms of perpetual mourning—mourning which went on until Victoria's death many years later. The wish to avoid the reality of his death is shown by the fact that even at that time Albert's clothes were being laid out every night, and hot water put in a bowl for him. This has been called by Geoffrey Gorer "fossilization", an attempt to keep the person who has died in fossilized form for ever after.

What can one do to help people through grief and to minimize the chances of these pathological reactions occurring? First of all, there is the opportunity to help prior to the bereavement itself. How can we help prepare people for loss? Is a blanket denial of an impending death the best way of coping? I believe opportunity should be taken more often to work with the dying and their families towards a realistic acceptance of the true situation. In some places a real attempt is made to work with the patient in this way; not to force him to face facts that he is not strong enough to accept, but to try to be around and help him to express what he wants to express. It is a process of working with a person, rather than doing something to him. And of course it is a situation in which the family can help, and in which it may help them to be involved.

CFF

When the bereavement itself occurs, clearly there are certain things happening which may help or hinder the widow. For instance, the psychological functions of the ritual of the funeral and mourning are often ignored. It is assumed that the funeral is somehow arranged primarily for the dead person. But it may in my opinion also be something of considerable importance to the widow herself. In so far as she needs people around who are able to share her grief and to help her by doing so, a funeral may prove a very valuable ritual. Widows often speak with great gratitude of the number of letters they have received, and the tokens of respect for their dead husband, as if they somehow shared the esteem which was represented by these letters and gifts. Strangely enough, no one ever writes a letter of condolence to a child. I consider this very sad, because children have the same need as adults to be noticed and helped through their grief. If there is uncertainty as to how the child will react, a letter of condolence can be sent to the mother who will probably choose to show it to her child. Such a message might also help her to talk to the child about what has happened and so enable him to share in her grief.

We can help the griever to grieve by encouraging the expression of his feelings of despair, anger, or guilt. People very often feel angry with God: "Why did he let this happen?" It is a temptation, if you are a religious person, to argue with them, and to force your view of God on to the bereaved person. Such a response fails to recognize the irrational component in the anger. In his book *A Grief Observed*, C. S. Lewis described his reaction to the death of his wife, and it is very plain that he too went through this feeling of intense anger towards God, which he expressed in his diary at that time. I think it is important that he had the courage to publish this book and to include the extracts in his diary in which he says just what he feels about God. Reading the book we can see how as time passed he was able to get back to a view of God which was not destructive or rejecting.

How do we help people to grieve? Often it is a matter of opening oneself to the bereaved; not browbeating them, or forcing them to talk about things they are afraid of, but just being around and attempting to reassure them of the normality of what is happening to them. A bereaved person will often say, "Look here, I'm going mad: it's not me—I don't have feelings like this—I never have . . .". Part of our problem in this situation is that we cannot give them the one thing that they really want—we can't bring back the person who has died. This means that we are saddled with a feeling of helplessness which it may be difficult for us to accept. But accept them we must. The bereaved person may want to make rash decisions—to dispose of everything, to sell the house, and so on. Under these circumstances it is important to bring home the fact that retreating from the situation in panic is not going to solve it, and that such actions may be deeply regretted later.

With the support of family and friends the widow can eventually be encouraged to find something fresh in life. Mourning is a duty as well as a need, and there sometimes comes a stage when the widow can be reminded that she has done her duty, and that it is all right to stop mourning—in that she can go out to parties and need not remain withdrawn from society. Many a widow will describe a "turning point" in her grief; maybe a special occasion, a holiday, or an anniversary. She will say, "Up to that moment I was thinking of the past, and then I went to my sister for a couple of weeks, and when I came back I thought 'Well, I am not going to let all that occur again', and I changed round the furniture of the front room and I started decorating' "—this is the sort of thing which one sometimes helps to bring about. Holidays of course are occasions which may very often be "turning points", provided they come at the right time. Trouble can arise when they become mere panicky escapes from a difficult and depressing situation. It may be necessary for a widow to go through a number of "turning points" before she begins to feel that she has discovered a new life. New roles are terribly important, and self-esteem resulting from involvement in work, in community activities, church groups, social clubs, and so on, can do much towards a successful working through of grief.

The value of belief in life after death for the bereaved is not easy to study. There is a great deal of difference, for instance, between formal religious observance and belief, and it is not always easy to recognize the genuine conviction. However, I would say that a large number of sincerely religious people who have a philosophy of life and a system of belief which goes really deep, and becomes part of them, are in some part already prepared when somebody dies. There is the feeling that death is itself something meaningful rather than just something that is "being done to me". This does not necessarily mean they have no need to grieve; although assured that they are going to meet the departed again, the present separation and parting can be extremely painful.

When should we seek for help in our pastoral care of the bereaved? Particularly dangerous is the threat of suicide. Fortunately acts of suicide are much less common than threats, but they do occur. A bereaved person will very often say, "I wouldn't care if I died tomorrow", but will very seldom do anything about it. However, if you are in any doubt, do not hesitate to get advice from the local general practitioner or perhaps a psychiatrist. Doctors and psychiatrists are often able to give valuable assistance, and there is need for them to learn that clergy and others in the community can be of help in this kind of situation.

5

The Theology of Forgiveness

C. F. D. Moule

t would be difficult to name an aspect of Christian theology that
s wider or more demanding than the theology of forgiveness.
To plumb its depths would require not only immense learning and
mature thought: it would require also an exceptionally wide
pastoral experience. Also, I believe that only he can speak authen-
ically about forgiveness who has himself been greatly forgiven;
and, however deeply I may need forgiveness, I do not believe that
have yet begun to understand more than the fringes of the
experience. On many counts, then, I am disqualified for anything
more than a fragment, at most, of this big task. But I accepted the
invitation gratefully because there is a thing that, I hope, I may be
able to do—namely, to contribute something towards the defini-
ion and clarification of one particular problem in the under-
tanding of forgiveness. It is a problem which happens to be a
pecial concern of mine, and I have more than once before ventured
no doubt rashly) into print about it,[1] and I am not loath to try
gain to present it. I believe it to be of considerable pastoral and
practical importance, though this will not, I fear, be immediately
vident. What I am going to say may well sound abstract and
cademic. But if you will bear with me I hope it will become clear
hat an understanding of the atonement and of our ministry of
reconciliation depends, in some degree at least, upon the clarity
vith which we grasp the issues in question.

[1] "Punishment and Retribution: an attempt to delimit their scope in New
Testament thought", *Svensk Exegetisk Årsbok*, xxx (1965), 21 ff.; "The
Christian Understanding of Forgiveness", *Theology*, lxxi. 580 (October 1968),
35 ff.

The problem I have in mind may be called that of compensation. Forgiveness is, by definition, free: it is an act of grace or mercy; it is a gift. Yet equally, it is very widely held that an offence requires to be paid for by the offender: repentance is costly. Is there, then, after all, a transaction involved in forgiveness, and is it a matter of barter?

The problem in question thus concerns the propriety of applying quantitative ideas (such as "cost") to the attempt to analyse the process of forgiveness and reconciliation. And here, as I see it, there are two principles in apparent tension against one another. On the one hand, it is a wholly inadequate—indeed, a stultifying and self-contradictory—notion of forgiveness that sees it as the settling of a credit and debit account, as though the offender paid and the injured party was then satisfied. That may be what happens when an offence is dealt with on the level of legal proceedings, but it is certainly remote from what happens on the level of personal relations when an estrangement is healed. On the other hand, sin seems to be so momentous and its results so objective that it is difficult to describe a breach of personal relationships without having recourse to the notion of a "quantum"—a measurable amount—of damage, which cannot be ignored, but has to be compensated by an equivalent amount of repair before it can be healed. Both these aspects of the matter concern personal relationship; but in the former case quantitative ideas of debt and payment are manifestly out of place; whereas in the latter case it is difficult to safeguard the objective seriousness of sin without quantitative language. The relation between two persons cannot be described quantitatively, and yet the measure of the offence somehow needs to be taken. I believe that a formula can be found which does justice to both these considerations and to the reality they attempt to describe, but I think that it needs careful definition; and I believe that the attempt to reach such definition does help to deepen understanding and to resolve some problems in the Christian interpretation of atonement. That is why I hope that, ultimately, this will be a great deal more than a merely academic inquiry. It will affect, in the last analysis, the theory and practice both of pastoral care and of legislation.

That a credit-and-debit way of speaking is out of place on the personal level of forgiveness, repentance, and reconciliation is obvious enough. Forgiveness, I repeat, is, by definition, free.

ndeed, the first and most difficult lesson that an offender has to earn is that he cannot deserve or earn forgiveness. Forgiveness would not be forgiveness if it were offered as a *quid pro quo*. The offender may make material reparation for any material damage he may have caused; but, if he is to be forgiven by the person he has offended against, he must be humble enough to accept the forgiveness *gratis* and not try to pretend he can earn it. This is exactly what St Paul's doctrine of justification by grace through faith is urging in regard to divine forgiveness. The response is by faith; but the offer is *gratis*, it is sheer generosity, it is grace. By the same token, there is (as far as I can see) no place at all in a Christian understanding of forgiveness for the forgiving person to indulge in retaliation, reprisals, or punishment, as such. The exclusion of punishment and its bracketing with retaliation and reprisals may surprise some of us. But I do exclude it, and rank it side by side with those others, because, ordinarily at least, the word "punishment" implies some satisfaction of abstract justice, over and above whatever infliction may be necessary for educating the offender or deterring him and others from repeating the offence. And, whereas a "penalty", in the commonly understood sense, may help to bring home to the offender his responsibility and to discourage further offences, the demand for satisfaction as such—the infliction of punishment in the name, not of education or deterrence but of retribution or abstract justice—seems to be quite outside the realm of the reconciliation of two persons.

Thus, on the level of the relationship itself between persons, quantitative ideas seem simply not appropriate—indeed, positively false. Forgiveness is not logical and quantitative: it is always a miracle of free grace. Tit for tat is no part of forgiveness and repentance—even if the *lex talionis* was originally a great advance beyond the jungle law of vendetta. On the other hand—and this is an important part of my contention—there appears to be as strict a natural law of cause and effect (still on the level of personal relations) as anywhere else—so strict that it does not seem inappropriate to describe it, albeit metaphorically, in terms of a sort of conservation of energy. It is as ineluctable as Karma or Nemesis. What I mean is that a breach of fellowship by some offence committed by one person against another is comparable to a quite objective—if you like, quantitative—disturbance of the total equilibrium. The destructive energy of sin—of a violation of a personal relationship—is something that cannot be counteracted except by the output of an equivalent energy of repair. The impact of the offence sends out ripples which must somehow, somewhere, be accounted for—either bounced back in retaliation, or else absorbed—if the equilibrium is to be restored. Or—to change the metaphor—the ravages of disease have to be countered by the corrective activity of all the leucocytes and lymphocytes and the rest of the militia that the body calls into action until the crisis is over. The process, in other words, is a matter of energy pitted against equivalent energy.

So there is our dilemma. On the one hand there is this doctrine of free, unconditional forgiveness, matched by a penitence which is humble enough to acknowledge that it cannot earn or pay for forgiveness—seemingly a most *un*-quantitative process; but on the other hand is the need for an estimate of the character of sin, so realistic and objective and serious, that it has to resort to analogies of the quantitative type in order to safeguard *quanti ponderis sit peccatum* (to quote the inevitable tag). And I suggest that it is the failure to bring these two considerations together into a single, realistic system that is partly responsible for the fact that different Christian theories of the atonement come into collision with one another. A crude doctrine of a feudal God who demands a penalty to be undergone by Jesus Christ as satisfaction, before he can forgive the sins of mankind, is monstrous and clearly unacceptable. But it is because any alternative may appear to be unrealistic in its estimate of the objective seriousness of sin that suspicion is apt to fall on theories which reject the penal element.

By way of attempting a single system which will do justice to the realities both of the mystery of free grace and of the measurable force and objective "quantum" that is sin, I suggest a distinction between motives and consequences or between the description of a relationship and the description of the activity of sin; and in the interests of this, a specialized use of the metaphor of cost and expenditure. The point is that sin does have to be "paid for": that is a true insight. But where we are apt to go wrong in the use of such quantitative terms is in assuming that the payment is bound to be made by the offender (or some representative, acting on his behalf) to the injured one; whereas, in fact, payment has to be made by both of them, the injured party and the offender, to—what shall we say?—God's own system of personal relationship. Forgiveness, real forgiveness, is undoubtedly costly to the forgiver: "it takes it out of you". Not that genuine forgiveness can ever be unwillingly offered or can ever have to be dragged out of a man: its essence is that it is an act of spontaneous generosity. The father of a prodigal son, if he is a real father, will run eagerly to meet him and will fling his arms round him. There is nothing quantitative in his motive. But that does not alter the fact that the forgiveness is costly. A generous person is, by definition, one who can feel keenly and who, therefore, can be hurt; and the readiness to forgive is not lightly won: it is part of a character that is subject to great depths of agony. Therefore, into the sheer joy and alacrity of the father's welcome to his son there has gone, and continues to go, any amount of costly pain and suffering and nervous energy, even though this is no conscious part of his intentions. Forgiveness uses you up. It is free, not because it costs nothing, but because the price is willingly, or perhaps even unconsciously, paid by the donor himself.

I hope this is a true account of what happens. If it is, then we are nearer to understanding the quantitative side of the description. As I said, personal relationships are seen to be subject to strict laws of cause and effect such that the impact of sin can only be neutralized by some compensatory action of equivalent weight. And forgiveness and repentance are both costly. Just as the wronged party will be less than his full self as a person if he retaliates and is not willing to pay for his gift of forgiveness, so the offender will be less than his full self if he does not wish to compensate. Notoriously, real repentance "feels like death". Repentance cannot take place except by the penitent's stooping low and losing all *amour propre* and giving up all thought of deserving forgiveness. And the very repudiation of all attempt to pay turns out (by a strange paradox) to be itself infinitely costly. It involves the painful confession, "I was wrong. Father, I have sinned: I don't deserve to be your son." Thus, strangely enough, although forgiveness is a costly gift, purchased by the donor and offered as a gift such as cannot be earned or purchased by the recipient with however costly a satisfaction, yet neither can it be accepted without the cost of the offender's self-esteem. He cannot purchase it for anything, but neither can he receive it as a gift without giving everything of himself. And more: a real forgiveness really received by true repentance means that the offender conceives a burning desire to make reparation and to share the burdens of the one who forgave him. The prodigal son, if he is really penitent, will share with his father in a costly, conciliatory appeal to the scornful elder brother. Though he cannot earn the forgiveness, yet the true penitent does expend all that he has. The original self-concern which, in the process of repentance, is transformed into a concern for the one he has injured, makes the penitent eager to lavish on the one who forgives him all that he has and is.

Thus a process of reconciliation which, by its very nature (being on a fully personal level), is quite beyond a nicely-calculated less or more, may nevertheless be well described (indeed, must be described) in terms of expenditure and cost. But it is not the cost of a debt paid by the debtor to a creditor. Payment does not enter into the motive or the description of the *relationship*. There is an act of free generosity, but it happens to be costly. And cost does enter into the description of the *process*. And there turns out to be a sacrificial output of energy on the other side of the dialogue also. The generosity of forgiveness which is ready to pay the full amount wakes, as it were, an echo from the recipient, and he too gives out all that he has in response. If, in this metaphor of cost or expenditure of energy, there is no transaction between the two parties, neither is there any question of there being a payment to some mythical recipient. This is not a rehabilitation of the crude theory of a ransom paid to the devil. It is not concerned with a decision to pay at all. That is why I said that a specialized use of the metaphor was called for. Rather, it is a physical metaphor of compensation. There is a "quantum" of energy needed to repair the breach, to restore equilibrium, to heal the disease. If there is payment to anything, it is a payment made by both sides to what I have already alluded to as that system which we believe to be God's own system, by which persons estranged find their full stature as persons reconciled by costly energizing.

Perhaps one might bring the two realms of thought—the non-quantitative and the quantitative—within a single system by saying that, on the personal level, the motive of forgiveness is always to heal and to restore the offender and never to "take it out of him" by punishment or reprisals or retaliation; and the motive of the true penitent is always to express his love and concern for the one he has injured, not to attempt to make himself worthy (which is impossible); but that, in fact, these two attitudes involve, albeit unconsciously and without any deliberate intention, a process which can only be described as one of balancing, of restoring the equilibrium, of absorbing poison, of neutralizing the disease—use what metaphors you will for the compensation. This would mean that a doctrine of free grace, involving no demand for distributive justice or reparation— indeed, repudiating it—is nevertheless no violation of what we normally call the justice of God, since, when we speak of the justice of God, what we really mean is that it is God's concern that every person should be brought to his full, undiminished stature as a son of God. And such regard for the full stature of personality involves a love which is realistic about the inexorable cost of things; a love which both forgives freely and also is too concerned for the offender's full, responsible personhood to spare him the pain of acknowledging his responsibility and rising to that personhood. It is a love which cuts no corners.

The appropriateness of quantitative language to the process is further illustrated by the very fact that several times already mention has been made of diminishing or enhancing personality. It is a diminution (we may intelligibly say), a reduction of a man's personality if he is not treated as a responsible person. Equally it is a diminution of the injured person's self if he nurses a grudge or demands reprisals or metes out punishment. The persons of both parties will be enhanced and brought to full stature precisely by the non-quantitative attitudes of unconditional, free forgiveness and unlimited repentance. In other words, the non-quantitative motives of personal relations and volition seem nevertheless to be inseparably linked to the quantitative consequences—the waxing and waning of personal stature.

Objectors to my plea for the elimination of punishment (so as to leave only education and deterrence as motives for the infliction of pain on the offender) have sometimes urged that the offender is, as a person, positively owed punishment; indeed, that offenders have been known to ask for punishment, because of an instinctive feeling that they cannot respect themselves again until they have been given what they deserve. In reply I would say that the offender, as a person, can never be owed punishment as such. As a precious, divinely-created person, he is owed only whatever will lift him to his full stature as a person; and, for that end, what is needed is not punishment (which, in ordinary usage at least, means the satisfaction of justice, the assignment of a suitable penalty, the exacting of satisfaction), but rather whatever will bring him to a free acknowledgement of his responsibility and a desire to meet it. This may be achieved by the infliction of pain; or it may be achieved by the refusal to inflict pain. In either case it will be by action aimed at something other than punishment or penalty or retribution or distributive justice, as these words are normally used. As for the offender's longing to recover his self-respect by being allowed to undergo punishment, that (strictly defined) is not the same thing as what I have been calling the desire to make reparation and the urge to give himself. The latter is outward-turned and is the result of true repentance and is a symptom of the humble acceptance of the free gift of pardon. It is essentially other-regarding. The former may be self-regarding, albeit with an enlightened self-regard. It is precisely what St Paul combats in his doctrine of justification by pure grace through faith.

Here I must acknowledge, in parenthesis, that I have been begging a vital question, namely, what is meant by "personality". I have been talking of the value of personality as an axiom, and speaking of the diminution of personal stature as axiomatically evil. But I am well aware that personality is a word that can too easily be used as a blank counter in a game without any proper definition. I can only plead that, for the purposes of this discussion, we know what we mean by the ability to be rightly related on the personal level. We can distinguish between autistic behaviour at one end and excessively dependent behaviour at the other. We can recognize, when we see it, a full, integrated personality, combining real independence and initiative with being open and humble towards others and able to live in community. And further, Christians believe that in a sense personality *is* a known entity, since in Jesus Christ the outlines of ideal human personality are revealed.

I turn now, at last and more briefly, to the more strictly theological side of the question. As I said, I am not competent to produce anything approaching a full-scale Christian theology of forgiveness; but I am naturally under an obligation to try to relate to the New Testament the assertions I have been making in more general terms about the structure of reconciliation.

My first point concerns God's initiative. Jesus, by the jealousy and fear of his opponents, was wrongly deprived—so the Christian interpreter believes—of his good name and of his life. Falsely accused of blasphemy before a Jewish court, and of sedition before Pilate, he was crucified. But (so Christians came to be convinced) the life of God asserted itself through and beyond that death. Subsequent Christian reflection on the events of Jesus' life and death, and on the extraordinary sequel, led to the conclusion that, in a unique sense, this had been God himself, submitting himself to man's ill will, and, by accepting it into himself, asserting his love as more powerful than man's hatred. St Paul saw it, on the titanic scale of the story of mankind collectively, as God's reply, in the ultimate Adam, to the first Adam's transgression. Man's first disobedience—the disobedience of the human race collectively—is met and reversed, not by retribution, but by the costly obedience of ultimate Man, who, while representing mankind collectively, is equally God himself at work in man:

> ... if the wrongdoing of that one man brought death upon so many, its effect is vastly exceeded by the grace of God and the gift that came to so many by the grace of the one man, Jesus Christ. . . . For if by the wrongdoing of that one man death established its reign, through a single sinner, much more shall those who receive in far greater measure God's grace, and his gift of righteousness, live and reign in the one man, Jesus Christ. . . . For as though the disobedience of the one man the many were made sinners, so through the obedience of the one man the many will be made righteous.
>
> Rom. 5.15–19 (N.E.B.).

Thus, in Jesus Christ, God himself is seen willingly and eagerly working out the pattern of his will, *in* and *through* the tragic, agonizing, infinitely painful circumstances created by man's self-concern. In other words, here is a realistic reckoning with the damage caused by sin—the breach, the alienation, between man and God; and the New Testament gospel declares that the cost of the repair is borne by God himself in Jesus Christ. So far from wreaking vengeance, God himself "absorbs" the evil: "God was in Christ reconciling the world unto himself" (2 Cor. 5.19). That the breach has caused concrete damage which must (so to speak) be "paid for" is also clear enough in the New Testament. The predicament of man cannot be met by a mere cease fire, or by a mere decision, like a "royal pardon", to ignore the wrong. Sin has got to be taken account of. The idea that an offence is, as it were, a "quantum" that must be disposed of is certainly at home in the New Testament, for instance, in Rom. 5 as just quoted. Quantitative metaphors are recognized by the New Testament. And the good news is that the slack is taken up (so to speak) by God himself, in Jesus Christ; or, if I may again resort to that physiological metaphor, the lesion in the body's tissue can be healed only by the output of creative energy. It is a sovereign act of the Creator. New creation is very much a Pauline idea: 2 Cor. 5.17; Gal. 6.15; Eph. 2.10; Col. 3.10.

Now, I have deliberately framed that statement in terms of God's initiative: God throughout is the subject of the verbs. And I do not believe that anyone will deny that this is true to the New Testament. But Jesus—so Christians believe—is man as well as God; and, if this act of repair is indeed God's act and at God's cost, yet it is carried out within man and, in Christ, it is offered up to God as the obedience of man to God, as the dutiful co-operation of a Son with his Father. This is the second point. Though it does not purchase God's forgiveness, it does express the Son's response of eager love (Eph. 5.2). And Christ, as the utterly obedient ultimate Adam, is in this sense the representative of man's costly repentance, as well as of God's costly forgiveness (see, again, Rom. 5.12 ff.). While Christ is (as Christians believe) in perfect harmony with his Father and acts for him towards men, his suffering also gathers and sums up the collective reparation which man must wish to offer to God as soon as man repents. Christ is the representative and "first fruits" of mankind's response to God's initiative. Thus in Christ, as he is understood on a more than merely individual scale, are effected simultaneously God's free forgiveness and man's costly repentance. As we have seen, the gracious free gift of God, in its very acceptance as a free gift, evokes the ultimate output of energy from responsive man. And in Christ the two sides of this reciprocal movement are already both a reality.

Now, once again, I believe that this account will be recognized as true to the New Testament, or at any rate to Paul; so that the heart of the New Testament gospel concerns a process of reconciliation such as I have been trying to define, a process which is immensely costly and demanding, but which involves no retribution or punishment, as such. But is it not a direct contradiction of this that the New Testament undoubtedly contains also a good deal about retribution? It was a widespread notion in Christianity

after the New Testament era that the fall of Jerusalem was divine
retribution on the Jews for deicide; and already in the Gospels
there are one or two hints that point in that direction—e.g. the
retribution on the insulting guests in the Matthean story of the
great feast (Matt. 22.7) and the strange coda to the Lucan story of
the money in trust (Luke 19.27). Moreover, "wrath" (*orge*) is
a familiar New Testament theme, especially in Paul and in the
Apocalypse; and, even if Paul's use is so specialized that a front-
rank New Testament scholar like C. H. Dodd can argue[1] that it does
not mean anger as an emotion against sinners but disaster as a
consequence of sin, this still (even if true) does not dispose of the
retributive motive from Paul's teaching. Rom. 2.6–11 is a very
explicit passage about retribution, and Rom. 1 and 2 as a whole
are full of the theme. *Orge* itself, indeed, is rendered by "retribution" in the N.E.B. at 1.18, 2.5, and (perhaps) 2.8.[2]

As for the Apocalypse, it is, in some places, vindictive in the
extreme (e.g. 16.5 f.). Similarly, the climax of certain of the
Gospel parables sounds retributive (Matt. 13.42, 50; 25.46; etc.).
The language of retaliation, then, and the idea of deserved punishment are not difficult to find in the New Testament.[3]

Formally, this is certainly a contradiction of what I have been
saying. And, although I believe that most of the apparent examples of retribution in the parables turn out, on closer inspec-
tion, to be picturesque ways of describing the inevitable results
of estrangement rather than God's intention to penalize, nevertheless there is enough in St Paul and the Apocalypse and a few
other places to prove that retribution and punishment formed part
of the system of thought accepted by these writers. But that is
almost inevitable, seeing that New Testament thought is largely
in the framework of Old Testament presuppositions, which give
much prominence to the portrayal of God as a God of justice,
vindicating his moral law by bringing retribution on the guilty.
This was itself a great advance on pagan ideas of venal gods who
had no consistency and in whose behaviour justice was no consideration—gods who had, in fact, no moral character at all. It
was one of the chief glories of the eighth-century Prophets of

[1] E.g. in *The Epistle of Paul to the Romans*. London: Hodder & Stoughton
1932, p. 29.
[2] And Rom. 1.27 uses the word *antimisthia*, "recompense".
[3] Details in *Svensk Exegetisk Årsbok*, as in n. 1, p. 61,

Israel that the God whom they preached had a consistent character; and it would have been virtually impossible for New Testament thinking not to have had a correspondingly juridical structure. What is remarkable, however, is the extent to which these axiomatic preconceptions have been modified by the Christian revelation. There is, as a matter of fact, extraordinarily little about punishment, properly so called, in the New Testament. Words which may be so translated are rare. Thought about wrath too has, at least in Paul, begun to be redirected. The sheer paradox of God's undeserved graciousness is so compelling that Paul's justification by grace through faith cuts away the ground from under the legalism that wrath ultimately implies. God is a God who puts the wicked right; who is content, in Jesus Christ, to suffer at the hands of the ungodly; who exercises his sovereign creative power by suffering, not by causing to suffer; who himself pays for the entail of sin instead of demanding satisfaction from the sinner. All in all, it is wrath and punishment which turn out to be the anomalies, in the full blaze of the New Testament gospel, not the other way round. It would thus appear that the implications of the New Testament gospel are to treat the consequences of sin quantitatively, but not to quantify relationship, which is what I was trying to argue in the first part of my discourse.

Now it is not for me to say what bearing all this may have in detail upon the pastoral ministry—especially the ministry to the sick. Nor have I even brought into view the agonizing problem of human beings who, for environmental or psychological or hereditary reasons, appear virtually to have ceased to come within the category of personality with which I have been exclusively working. I have not made reference to the work of Dr Frank Lake and others on the psychology of forgiveness and penitence, and I have left aside all sorts of other relevant literature, including that notable study *The Ethics of Punishment*, by Sir Walter Moberly.[1] But because I believe that a false evaluation of the problem of compensation, as I have called it, distorts atonement doctrine and the interpretation of absolution and penance, and therefore vitiates our ministry of reconciliation, I venture to hope that even this very limited study of it is not wholly irrelevant to the intention of this series of studies.

[1] London: Faber & Faber 1968.

6

The Theology of Wholeness

Ian Ramsey, Bishop of Durham

In a book published some seventeen years ago based on lectures which had been given in Oxford almost ten years earlier, Miss Phyllis L. Garlick singles out "wholeness" as the idea whose time has come. The book, *Man's Search for Health*, followed two other volumes which Miss Garlick had written, one of whose titles was, significantly for our purpose, *The Wholeness of Man: A Study in the History of Healing*. All those books had been published seventeen years ago, so I think Miss Garlick's welcome to the idea of wholeness was somewhat premature for only very slowly has it coloured our thought and practice in relation to human beings and their health.

I

As is well-known, wholeness is certainly not an idea which has always been a presupposition of medical care or of philosophical and theological thinking, nor could it be said to be the popular idea of human personality. There is the well-known hymn which speaks of body and soul meeting again on the Resurrection morning. There is the Compline prayer which asks "that when our bodies lie in the dust, our souls may live with thee". I am not saying, of course, that these phrases ought never to be used; I am not saying that they cannot be given a logical unpacking that is different from that which their verbal form might suggest. Indeed, that is my point. For I fear that their verbal form has often misled people into supposing that human personality was a compound made up of two constituents: a body and a soul.

Significantly, and helpfully it seems to me, in the service of Holy Communion the phrase "our souls and bodies" is only given as a further and subsequent specification of the word which precedes it, namely "ourselves". This seems to me to be a kind of philosophical high water-mark in liturgical expression. To some extent, the very words we use in conversation perpetuate the notion of a dichotomy. For example, we speak, say, of Mr Jones going up the mountain, but after a fatal accident we speak of Mr Jones's body being brought down. In other words, there is certainly a very great deal in conversation and in language generally to support Professor Gilbert Ryle's view that

> There is a doctrine about the nature and place of minds, which is so prevalent among theorists and even among laymen that it deserves to be described as the official theory . . . The official doctrine, which hails chiefly from Descartes, is something like this. . . . With [a few] doubtful exceptions . . . every human being has both a body and a mind. Some would prefer to say that every human being is both a body and a mind. His body and his mind are ordinarily harnessed together, but after the death of his body his mind may continue to exist and function.

To such a theory, Ryle contends, "most philosophers, psychologists, and religious teachers subscribe with minor reservations".[1]

How far we may rightly lay the responsibility for this theory at the door of Descartes is another matter, and it will I think be worth our while to spend a little longer on Descartes and the views he inherited.

The late Dr Austin Farrer remarks in his book *The Freedom of the Will* (A. & C. Black 1958):

> For the picture of body and mind which Descartes inherited, we may turn to Aristotle *On the Soul*. In that treatise the philosopher had profited (we may think) from the ambiguities of the Greek word *psyche*, with its double sense of *life* and *consciousness*. The body is alive, and therefore "ensouled"; that is, it has the principles of action which are proper to animal life, whether conscious or otherwise.[2]

Dr Farrer continues:

Descartes grew up in an Aristotelian world, but there was one feature of the Aristotelian picture that he could not stomach: the ruthless

[1] *The Concept of Mind.* Hutchinson 1949, p. 11.   [2] Op. cit., pp. 14–15.

uniformity of his new physics demanded that the human body should be interpreted as physical clockwork. . . . The actual power of moving the bodily parts must be credited to bodily clockwork; all immediate feeling of bodily state and motion must be credited to the godlike thinking soul or mind, which is now left as the only soul there is. Descartes was not synthesizing science and common-sense and common experience; he was hashing Aristotle. . . . Descartes was not so much authoritative, as typical.[1]

Some forty years earlier the pioneer psychologist James Ward had also related Aristotle and Descartes. He says, "So far Aristotle's point of view resembles that of modern-day biologists. His conception of soul has few of its present-day associations, while it is closely related to the physiological conception of function."[2] Aristotle; as we have seen, had certainly a concept of "wholeness", but it was the wholeness of a biological organism, and therefore it is not at all surprising that in medieval times the Aristotelian psychology had developed into a hazy materialism. "This," says James Ward, "Descartes banished once for all by the new definitions he gave of matter and mind."[3] Aristotle found mind and body invariably connected and therefore he, Aristotle, regarded them as essentially inseparable. Descartes could conceive of mind and body and body without mind. Therefore, he concluded, they were actually independent and could exist apart. So we arrive at Cartesian dualism.

That Descartes himself could not regard this as the full story is clear from *Meditation vi*, when he remarks:

> Nature also teaches me by these sensations of pain, hunger, thirst, etc., that I am not only lodged in my body as a pilot in a vessel, but that I am very closely united in it and, so to speak, so intermingled with it that I seem to compose with it one whole.[4]

And in that same *Meditation* a few sentences later he speaks of the union and apparent intermingling of mind and body. But how for Descartes was such a substantial unity, such a "wholeness", possible?

[1] Op. cit., p. 16.
[2] *Psychological Principles*. C.U.P. 1918, pp. 2, 3.
[3] Op. cit., 6.
[4] *The Philosophical Works of Descartes*. E.T., Haldane and Ross, i, C.U.P., 1931, p. 192.

The two were linked together, he himself suggested elsewhere, at the pineal gland, thought of as a point, for a point has an affinity with matter, being part of an extended area, yet it is something not itself extended and therefore has an affinity to mind. The most Descartes could do for the unity, the wholeness, of the personality was to regard the pineal gland as a mathematical point effecting some kind of unification of the body and mind. But even if we give Descartes credit for his second thoughts and credit for his ingenuity, it is quite plain that the concept of wholeness is now a compound concept, made up of mind and body as constituent elements. By contrast, however inadequate was Aristotle's notion of human personality and however much it could be regarded as materialistic—and was so interpreted— at least Aristotle's concept presupposed genuine wholeness as its basic category, whereas for Descartes, the basic categories were "mind" and "body". Yet, however unfortunate the dualism which he fathered, Descartes' merit over Aristotle was that he was trying, one way or another, to avoid Aristotle's materialism. The theology of wholeness, I shall suggest, must be such as links Aristotle's notion of an active organism, a whole totality, with that notion of personal transcendence which I believe Descartes was trying to preserve, albeit badly, by his dichotomy of mind and body.

Meanwhile, let us not too easily contrast Hebrew and Greek thinking in these respects. I have argued that Aristotle, none other than a Greek philosopher, came far closer to ideas of wholeness than did Descartes. Indeed, those who complain that Greek philosophy encouraged dualism, must certainly be thinking more of Plato than Aristotle, and then be over-simplifying Plato at that.[1]

[1] It is true for example, that in the *Phaedo*, a treatise on immortality, Plato does contrast the divine and enduring soul, which shares in the eternal forms, with the mutable human body which belongs to the flux of change and the pattern of becoming. The contrast between mind or soul and body, which we find in Plato, is certainly one which matches entirely Plato's contrast between the world of sense and everyday experience on the one hand, and a higher world of ideas and forms which are eternal on the other. Even so, in very many ways it would be far more reliable to claim that dualism is encouraged by Latin rather than Greek ways of thinking: cf. L. W. Grensted, "The changing background of theological studies", *Bulletin of the John Rylands Library*, xxxvii, 1954, 33, 36):
The difference between the Latin and Greek approaches may be readily

II

So much for an outline of some of the metaphysical ancestry of the idea of wholeness. In order now to show how the theology of wholeness illuminates, brings coherence to, and provides a background for medical thought and practice, let me first say something, inevitably amateur, as to how medical science itself comes to think naturally in terms of unities—in terms of wholeness of man.

I need say very little about the development of psychosomatic illnesses which provide a crushing blow from the medical side to any Cartesian dualism or separatism: "the official doctrine", as Ryle called it. For here, in psychosomatic illnesses, are phenomena, of which perhaps asthma and some arthritic and rheumatic disorders are examples, which cannot be properly treated, either in terms of mental events alone, or bodily events alone. They certainly presuppose far more of a correlation and link between the two than could ever be provided for by that minimum unity —that point-gland—which Descartes even at his best could not get beyond. But by now we can draw examples from an even wider field. For when we look at the kind of thing which the medical sciences now say about the human personality, we find that time and time again we are pointed to the unity of that personality. We are pointed, within medicine, in the direction of the concept of wholeness.

Let me give some examples. Those who are concerned with the various understandings of personality now available to the biological sciences, come to regard the personality—and I believe rightly—as a complex matrix of interacting factors: some psychological, some biochemical, some endocrine, whether inborn or acquired, and there are as well no doubt many other factors as yet unknown. More particularly, in a psychological illness a

seen by noting the familiar phrase *mens sana in corpore sano*—a sound mind in a sound body—cannot be translated directly into Greek at all. . . . The terms of Greek philosophy became in the fourth and fifth centuries fitted to the usages of common Christian speech with the legalists and the administrators of the Latin West struggling to keep pace with their thought; failing again and again to appreciate its deeper reality of meaning and thinking all the time that they were leading the way.

vicious circle may and does arise between factors called respectively "functional" and "organic". The functional factors would be the psychological ones; the organic factors might be, for instance, endocrine, biochemical, physiological, and they may be externally controlled, as for example, by the use of drugs. Now abnormalities in any of these factors—functional or organic—may start an illness, and by the time the patient seeks professional help, both sides are usually active. Here is the vicious circle. We may start with functional disorders and find an organic problem as well; we may start with an organic factor and find a psychological illness as well. In other words, illness, like health, comes to be seen as a function of many factors, some of which have been traditionally associated with the mind, others with the body. But to speak in this way of health and illness as being a function of many variables, is only another way (by means of a concept of overall correlation, and using in particular the mathematical model of variables related by a function) of approaching the concept of wholeness.

Only on this kind of background, where there is a concept of wholeness, do we begin to understand why either organic or psychological treatment of psychological illness may be partially effective, and why perhaps both kinds of treatment will often, if not normally, be required. For example, in *anorexia nervosa*, psychotherapy along with drug and dietary treatment may both be beneficial. Or again, that health and illness alike, are functions of both psychological and physical factors can be seen by recalling how Freud, influenced by a background of anatomy and neurology, tried for many years to accommodate mental illness to the mechanistic model of disease; the kind of model which would be encouraged by the dualism associated with Descartes. It was only after several years of experience with patients suffering from mental disorders, that Freud arrived at the conclusion that brain disfunction alone was not sufficient to explain the mental disorders of patients who came to him. It may, or may not, be that Freud, like many other pioneers, went far in the opposite direction. All I am saying at the moment is that we have come increasingly to see that mental disorders very often, if not always, have physical concomitants as well, and to have both variables involved points to a unifying function, to the unity, the wholeness, of the person who is diseased.

Yet again, for the medical side, personality is sometimes understood in terms of adaptability in meeting external stresses. On this view, personality would reside in the capacity of a person to come to terms with outside buffets, to assert himself actively in relation to that stress which is an attack upon the subject by active external forces, which render that subject relatively passive and so lead to disease, dis-ease. Mental health and personality in this kind of context—the context of stress, stress illnesses—presuppose adaptability, and adaptability is another way of styling unity. The more a man or a woman shows wholeness, the more adaptable he is in relation to external forces.

Now in those ways and in many others medicine points us to a concept of personality as a unity. And something of that same conclusion is reached when, for example, we picture the pituitary gland as what has been called the conductor of the endocrine orchestra. Obviously the metaphor points to some kind of presiding unity. Or when we speak of the brain, as neurologists rightly would, as one of the best self-regulated mechanisms in the universe, this again points us in the direction of unity. In this way and many others medicine in a therapeutic context points us to a unity of personality, and a concept of wholeness.

And so at last we come to the heart of our topic. Can theology supply a wider framework, some interpretative scheme which is coherent with this kind of medical thinking? Can this medical viewpoint be set within a Christian perspective? Are there theological concepts which can integrate the fragmented knowledge of personality which is given by biochemistry, endocrinology, psychology, psychiatry, and the rest? It is because psychology and biology are closely linked today that we are likely to find ourselves closer to Aristotle than to Descartes, though we must share Descartes' dislike of reductionism. In other words, can the Aristotelian notion of an active soul, an active organism, be given a setting which is both Christianly and medically up to date?

To this question we can now turn.

III

Let us go back first to the origins of the Christian faith in the Old Testament, and in particular to the earliest account of the Creation of Man which we find in the first creation narrative of Genesis, the one to be found in chapter 2, where in verse 7 we read: "And the Lord God formed man of the dust of the ground and breathed into his nostrils the breath of life and man became a living soul." Here certainly was man considered as a unity with personality, as a wholeness; an ensouled body, if you like, or an embodied soul if you want to put it the other way round. The basic concept of Genesis 2.7 is enshrined in that Hebrew word *nepesh* which can mean interchangeably breath or life, soul or mind, but also living being, creature, person, and self. Secondly, and though the incident is not given to us as a theory of personality, an important view of personality is implied in the Ezekiel parable of the valley of dry bones (Ezekiel 37). In this picture, you remember, the bones came together, bone to his bone—a kind of anatomical demonstration—and then there were sinews upon them, and the flesh came up and skin covered them above. But, we are told in verse 8; "There was no breath in them". So significantly, "Thus saith the Lord God; come from the four winds, O breath, and breathe upon these slain, that they may live". In other words, those bodies, physiologically and anatomically considered, needed not to have some extra object added, put in the middle of them, as though they were some kind of ethereal dumpling. What they wanted was the enlivening, activating breath, wind, or spirit in order that they might live; and the activating breath or spirit of God is an activity that embraces and reaches over not only the temporal but the eternal as well. It was in exercising the activity, derived from the spirit of God within them, that those bodies knew and realized their transcendence, their faith-dimension, their dimension of the eternal; no question of reductionism here. Here is the wholeness of personality spelt out in terms of spirit and wind and breath; not in terms of various objects, but activity. But it goes further than Aristotle in having a transcendent reference.

The Christian view of man builds upon that idea of man we have already seen to be in the Old Testament. The specifically Christian answer to the question "What is Man?" or rather "What may Man be?" is given by reference to the disclosure of God's love in Christ. It is in responding to that love of God in Christ, responding to that love with a total commitment, that the Christian becomes the new creature and, whatever he does, he does all to the glory of God, responding to a disclosure of God in love and glory; e.g. Colossians 3.17. Putting the point in a little more detail from another epistle (1 Cor.), there is for St Paul for instance, at least in theory, the natural man; the man who is nothing beyond a combined topic of the natural, medical, and behavioural sciences—the natural man. Here is the man who receiveth not the things of the spirit of God (1 Cor. 2.14), whose life is restricted to the natural world, who in one sense does not live as distinct from existing; and by contrast to this natural man there is the spiritual man, the man who discerns the things of the spirit of God, which we may translate alternatively: is braced by the wind of God blowing in his face; who responds to the activity of God disclosed in Christ; who sees the deep things of God, things which are known in a disclosure situation of depth. Here is the spiritual man who finds life and freedom, wholeness, and health in responding to what he discerns in depth. This is the man who is saved, who is made whole, who has found himself in a response to a vision of God's love in Christ.

Words like "body" and "mind" and "spirit", while being three nouns and in that way similar in verbal form, have not at all for the Christian the same kind of logic. The word *body* refers to the physical organism to which all of us can point, and you cannot get more than half a dozen of them in a lift. A body is that through which each of us expresses himself, that which enables a philosopher like G. F. Stout to speak of an embodied self.[1] Alternatively, as I remarked earlier, some have spoken of an ensouled body.

What, secondly, is the *mind*? No counterpart object. We can most easily answer that question by saying "It is myself as thinking", or "Myself as remembering", or "Myself as solving the problem", when we think away the bodily aspects of that exercise. We are leaving it quite open as to how these particular actions in their totality are going to be analysed. Thirdly, what is the meaning of the word "*spirit*"? Spirit again is not some "thing"; it is that uniting activity with a transcendent God-given reference which makes both body and mind—and I underline the fact that these are not counterparts—"mine". It makes my thinking mine and my lying on the grass mine; the one done by the so-called body, the other done by the so-called mind. My

[1] *Mind and Matter*, G. How Lutuns, C.U.P., 1931.

body and my mind are expressions of me, of my activity. And we may here recall James Ward's point, that it is conation and not cognition which must be taken as the definitive account of the self. As Ware says on pp. 20–1 of *Psychological Principles*, "The sole function of perception and intellection is to guide action and subserve volition". He has said earlier, "Not intellect but will, not cognition but conation, not sensitivity . . . but activity, is the clue to a true understanding of the character and development of experience".

At death, what happens on this view is that my activity ceases to be expressed through that organism and behaviour pattern, through which in this spatial-temporal order it has been expressed hithertofore. The Christian view is that this activity which is definitively ourselves is then expressed elsewhere and in other contexts, about which on the whole the fewer details the better.

What this means is that concepts such as body and mind, body and soul are to be subsumed under the concept of person, that activity which informs our very being, that which makes each of us himself or herself.[1]

At this point, however, and for the sake of clarity, we must distinguish between two senses of active. In one sense we are active even when things are happening to us in which we have no spontaneous part. But this has been distinguished from those occasions when we are active with ourselves informing that activity. For instance, this is the case when I respond freely and spontaneously to some disclosed obligation; when I accept some challenge to which I freely respond; when I say I am inspired. That is a sense of activity altogether different from my activity when I tumble downstairs or fall off the bus: that is behavioural activity, it has not my personal backing—unless of course I am doing it in some comedy show. The theology of wholeness suggests that we take not just wholeness, but activity as our dominant concept, yet activity not as something which happens to me, but as that through which I express myself; the activity

[1] Cf. Gilbert Ryle, *The Concept of Mind*. Hutchinson 1949, pp. 50–1. "When *a person* talks sense aloud, ties knots, feints or sculpts . . . he is bodily active and he is mentally active, but he is not being synchronously active in two different 'places', or with two different 'engines'. Then is the *one activity*." (Italics mine.)

which has my personal backing; the activity which ranges over the whole area and integrates every aspect of our existence. Such activity is that which results from my free and spontaneous response to whatever is disclosed, whether it be a moral claim or a disclosure of God's love in Christ. And further, because as I have said, activity in this context involves a transcendent dimension, we have in the end a Christian baptism of Aristotle and avoid reductionism. In this connection perhaps I should issue a warning which has been implicit at a number of points, viz. that the concept of wholeness as used in biology and medical sciences, must never be given too naïve or uncritical a welcome. For between a purely biological wholeness and a wholeness interpreted in terms of transcendent activity there is just as serious and significant a gap as that which Descartes created between mind and body. In the long run, both imply that major difference between atheism and a belief in God.

So to restore physical health it is not enough to restore some upset equilibrium of the body; a cure must make it possible, as far as ever it can for our total activity to be freely expressed through that body. Or again, in the case of mental illness, the treatment must be such that through our thinking and remembering and our solving of problems and adapting ourselves to stress, our activity becomes more spontaneously and totally expressed. Here then, is a theology of wholeness. It can be a theology of caring, and I have tried to show it is coherent with the most significant terms, God and Christ, of our whole theological framework. For, as I have said, we discover this spontaneous activity, this which makes each of us distinctly ourselves by responding to a disclosure of God in Christ. There is nothing here which is authoritarian; nothing here dogmatically oppressive; nothing here judgemental in a bad sense. Rather this is a view of theology as mediating redeeming love and reconciliation and providing that milieu, that atmosphere, that climate in which men find wholeness in the sense of a widely-ranging, spontaneous activity in which they themselves are thoroughly involved. To talk of such activity is, of course, only another way of talking about freedom and life and fulfilment.

What then have I tried to do? A very brief summary. I have argued that there can be no adequate account of human personality, except by taking wholeness as a definitive category. That was the insight of Aristotle, an insight to be found in Hebrew thought, though by no means foreign to Greek ways of thinking. And not even Descartes could neglect it. Secondly, medical science, I have argued, points in the same direction in so far as either health or illness is seen to be a function of many factors; a matter of harmony between several variables, pointing us to the concept of the person as a unity. But it is important to avoid a materialistic reductionism and to preserve the element of transcendence which Cartesian dualism so misleadingly expressed. Thirdly, for the Christian, this wholeness is to be found in the response to the disclosure of God in Christ, a response which, made to love in freedom and spontaneity, brings to man life and fulfilment, a self-realization expressing itself through our biochemistry and our behaviour in so far as we can be healthy. This personal activity, however, will never in time be perfectly expressed, for we are, like the Author of our salvation, made perfect only through suffering and death, and perfect wholeness is but one way of styling our eternity.

FOR FURTHER READING

C. S. LEWIS
The Problem of Pain. Bles 1940

H. MERSKEY AND F. G. SPEAR
Pain: Psychological and Psychiatric Aspects. Baillière, Tindall & Cassell 1967

R. A. STERNBACH
Pain: A Psychophysiological Analysis. Academic Press (New York) 1968

W. F. ADAMS AND G. SHAW
Triumphant in Suffering: A Study in Reparation. Mowbrays 1951

TEILHARD DE CHARDIN
Le Milieu Divin. Collins 1960

J. HINTON
Dying. Penguin 1967

A. J. TOYNBEE, ED.
Man's Concern with Death. Hodder & Stoughton 1968

DAVID L. EDWARDS
The Last Things Now. S.C.M. Centrebooks 1969

L. BOROS
Moment of Truth. Burns & Oates 1965

GEOFFREY GORER
Death, Grief, Mourning in Contemporary Britain. Cresset Press 1965

NORMAN AUTTON
The Pastoral Care of the Dying. S.P.C.K. 1966

NORMAN AUTTON
The Pastoral Care of the Bereaved. S.P.C.K. 1967

C. S. LEWIS
A Grief Observed. Faber 1961

GILBERT COPE, ED.
Dying Death and Disposal. S.P.C.K. 1970

VINCENT TAYLOR
Forgiveness and Reconciliation. Macmillan 1946

L. HODGSON
The Doctrine of the Atonement. Nisbet 1951

GILBERT RYLE
The Concept of Mind. Hutchinson 1949

AUSTIN FARRER
The Freedom of the Will. Black 1958

I. T. RAMSEY, ED.
Biology and Personality. Blackwell 1965

JOHN MACMURRAY
The Self as Agent. Faber 1957

H. D. LEWIS
The Elusive Mind. Allen & Unwin 1969

DAVID JENKINS
The Glory of Man. S.C.M. 1967

ARTICLES

G. L. ENGLE
Psychogenic Pain and the Pain Prone Patient. *American Journal of Psychiatry*, 26 (1959), 899

C. SAUNDERS
The Management of Terminal Illness. *Hospital Medicine*, December 1966

E. STENGEL
Pain and the Psychiatrist. *British Journal of Psychiatry*, 111 (1965), 795

JOHN S. HABGOOD
Guilt and Forgiveness. *Theology*, September 1968

C. F. D. MOULE
The Christian Understanding of Forgiveness. *Theology*, October 1968

J. DOMINIAN
Forgiveness and Personality. *Theology*, November 1968

PETER WALKER
The Ministry of Forgiveness. *Theology*, December 1968